The **STDs** Update

Alvin and Virginia Silverstein and Laura Silverstein Nunn

Titles in the DISEASE UPDATE series:

DISEASE
UPDATE

The **STDs** Update

Alvin and Virginia Silverstein and Laura Silverstein Nunn

Enslow Publishers, Inc.

40 Industrial Road	PO Box 38
Box 398	Aldershot
Berkeley Heights, NJ 07922	Hants GU12 6BP
USA	UK

http://www.enslow.com

Acknowledgments

The authors thank Dr. Robert Johnson of the University of Medicine and Dentistry of New Jersey and Dr. Emilia Koumans of the Centers for Disease Control and Prevention for their careful reading of the manuscript and their many helpful comments and suggestions.

Library of Congress Cataloging-in-Publication Data

Silverstein, Alvin.
    The STDs update / Alvin and Virginia Silverstein
and Laura Silverstein Nunn. — 1st ed.
      p. cm. — (Disease update)
    Includes bibliographical references and index.
    ISBN-10: 0-7660-2484-9 (hardcover)
    1. Sexually transmitted diseases—Juvenile literature. I. Silverstein, Virginia B.
II. Nunn, Laura Silverstein. III. Title. IV. Series.
    RC200.25.S55 2005
    616.95'1—dc22

                        2005005990

ISBN-13: 978-0-7660-2484-7

Printed in the United States of America

10 9 8 7 6 5 4 3

To Our Readers: We have done our best to make sure all Internet Addresses in this book were active and appropriate when we went to press. However, the author and the publisher have no control over and assume no liability for the material available on those Internet sites or on other Web sites they may link to. Any comments or suggestions can be sent by e-mail to comments@enslow.com or to the address on the back cover.

Photo Credits: © 2005 Jupiter Images Corporation, pp. 8, 14, 23, 48, 65, 69, 102; BSIP / Photo Researchers, 103; Centers for Disease Control and Prevention (CDC), p. 10, 25, 28, 31, 46, 52, 60; Chris Bjornberg / Photo Researchers, Inc., 34; CNRI / Photo Researchers, Inc., p. 16; Cordelia Molloy / Photo Researchers, Inc., p. 36; Aid For AIDS, p. 78; Edwige / Photo Researchers, Inc., p. 35; Eye of Science / Photo Researchers, Inc., p. 62, 90, 93; Hank Morgan / Photo Researchers, Inc., p. 100; Kent Wood / Photo Researchers, Inc., p. 32; Laurent / Meeus / American Hospital of Paris / Photo Researchers, Inc., p. 58; Life Art image copyright 1998 Lippincott Williams & Wilkins. All rights reserved., pp. 19, 21, 63, 85; National Library of Medicine, p. 17; Paul Parker / Photo Researchers, Inc., p. 92; Picture Courtesy of the Soul City Institute For Health And Development Communication, p. 74; Saturn Stills / Photo Researchers, Inc., p. 98; Science Source, p. 42; Wellcome Library, London, p. 55.

Cover Photos: Cover photos: *top left:* Chris Bjornberg / Photo Researchers, Inc.; *others:* Eye of Science / Photo Researchers, Inc. Pictured (*clockwise from top left*) are colorized, microscopic images of: syphilis bacterium, trichomoniasis protozoan, herpes virus, and pubic lice, adult.

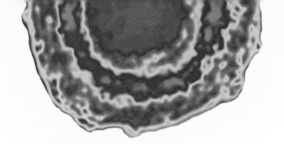

Contents

Sexually Transmitted Diseases

What are they?
Diseases that can be transmitted through sexual contact. Some may also be transmitted in nonsexual ways, such as through contact with blood, or from an infected mother to her unborn child.

Who gets them?
People of both sexes who are sexually active. Teens and young adults are most at risk because they are more likely to have sex with multiple partners. Newborns can catch the disease if their mother has it.

How do you get them?
Through sexual contact in the form of vaginal, anal, or oral sex. STDs may also be passed from an infected mother to her newborn. Contaminated needles used for injecting drugs, tattooing, or body piercing can spread HIV and hepatitis B.

What are the symptoms?
Depending on the type of STD, symptoms may include sores or rashes on the genitals, unusual fluids coming from the penis or vagina, itching, painful urination, or pain in the lower abdomen. In many cases, there are no obvious symptoms.

How are they treated?
Bacterial and fungal infections can be treated with antibiotics. Many viral diseases are incurable; symptoms can be eased with antiviral drugs. Pubic lice are killed with special creams and ointments.

How can they be prevented?
Avoiding all sexual contact or contact with the blood or other bodily fluids of an infected person. Using a condom during sexual activity can greatly reduce the risk of infection.

More than half of the new cases of STDs in the United States occur in people under the age of twenty-five. Young people should be aware of the risks and symptoms of these diseases.

1

What's Wrong with Sex?

EARLY IN 1999, twenty-year-old Anna wanted to get birth control pills. First, she had to take some routine tests at a sexually transmitted diseases clinic in Wake County, North Carolina. Anna felt good and had no complaints of any health problems, so she was not worried about the results.

When Anna went back to pick up her birth control pills, she was shocked. The tests showed that she was infected with a sexually transmitted disease called chlamydia. But how could she be sick? She felt perfectly fine. She didn't have any symptoms.[1]

Chlamydia is known as the "silent disease." Often there are no telltale signs of trouble. In fact, most people don't even know when they are infected. But if chlamydia is left untreated, it might damage a female's reproductive organs and make her unable to have children. Fortunately, this outcome is not very common.

What Are STDs?

Years ago, sexually transmitted diseases were known as venereal diseases, or VD for short. (The term *venereal* comes from *Venus*, the Roman goddess of love.) Now

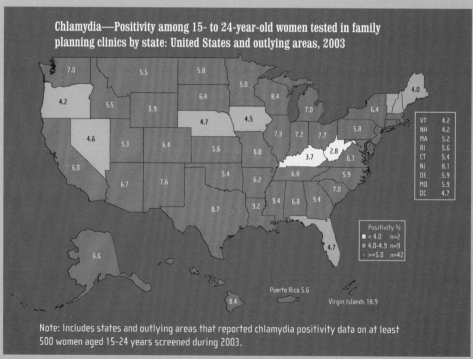

Chlamydia—Positivity among 15- to 24-year-old women tested in family planning clinics by state: United States and outlying areas, 2003

VT	4.2
NH	4.2
MA	5.2
RI	5.6
CT	5.4
NJ	8.1
DE	5.9
MD	5.9
DC	4.7

Positivity %
■ < 4.0   n=2
■ 4.0-4.9 n=9
□ >=5.0 n=42

Puerto Rico 5.6

Virgin Islands 18.9

Note: Includes states and outlying areas that reported chlamydia positivity data on at least 500 women aged 15-24 years screened during 2003.

This map shows the percent of people who tested positive for chlamydia in family planning clinics across the United States in 2003. Anna went to a North Carolina clinic for birth control pills, but found out she had chlamydia.

they are often called STDs, short for *sexually transmitted diseases*. Some medical experts prefer to call them STIs, for *sexually transmitted infections*.

There are more than twenty-five different kinds of STDs. They may be caused by a variety of creatures, ranging from tiny germs to insects. The one thing that STDs do have in common is that they are usually spread from person to person through sexual contact. Some people infected with an STD may not show any symptoms for months, years, or even for the rest of their lives. These people are known as carriers. They can spread the disease and not even know it. Having sex with a carrier does not guarantee the spread of the disease, but the more sex partners a person has, the greater the chances of getting an STD.

> More than 15 million new cases of STDs are reported in the United States every year. Two-thirds of them occur in people under the age of twenty-five, a quarter of them in teenagers.

Many young people are being exposed to STDs. More than 15 million new cases of STDs are reported in the United States every year. Two-thirds of them occur in people under the age of twenty-five, a quarter of them in teenagers.[2] Nearly one in five Americans needs

The Main Types of STDs

Name of STD	What Causes It?	Symptoms
AIDS	Virus	<u>Early:</u> none or fever and flulike symptoms. <u>Later:</u> night sweats, fatigue, swollen lymph nodes, mental confusion, weight loss, infections
Chlamydia	Bacterium	None at first. <u>Later:</u> (in 20% of females) vaginal itching and burning, yellow vaginal fluid (discharge), painful urination; (in 50% of males) watery, milky discharge; painful urination
Genital warts	Virus	Painless bumps on sex organs (many have no symptoms)
Gonorrhea	Bacterium	Burning with urination, discharge, pelvic pain (many have no symptoms)
Hepatitis	Virus	Nausea, yellowing of the skin, diarrhea
Herpes	Virus	Painful sores on the skin (many have no symptoms)
Pubic lice (crabs)	Insects	Genital itching
Syphilis	Bacterium	<u>Early:</u> sores on mouth or sex organs, fever, sore throat, headache, loss of appetite. <u>Later:</u> heart and nervous system problems
Trichomoniasis	Protozoan	Genital itching, redness, discharge (many have no symptoms)

to be treated for an STD by the time he or she reaches the age of twenty-one.[3]

> People do not like to talk about STDs, and especially to admit that they have one. This is one of the main reasons why STDs spread so easily.

Most people have heard a lot about AIDS, the deadliest of the STDs, on TV and in newspapers. Billions of dollars have gone toward AIDS research. Other STDs have hardly received any media attention and often go unnoticed. Some of these "forgotten" diseases can be dangerous or even deadly if they are not treated. STDs can lead to cervical cancer, infertility, and infant death.

Talking About S-E-X

Sexually transmitted diseases are a big problem all around the world. Worldwide, roughly 250 million people are infected with an STD.[4]

People do not like to talk about STDs, and especially to admit that they have one. This is one of the main reasons why STDs spread so easily. People who have an

STD may be shy about getting treatment, fearing that others might find out. They may also be ashamed to tell the people they might have infected. And their partners, in turn, might not realize they have an STD and go on to infect others.

A number of STDs are not curable, so drugs are not the answer. The key is prevention. People need to talk openly about sex and the dangers associated with it. By educating themselves, they can lessen their chances of getting infected and infecting someone else.

Is It *Really* an STD?

An icky discharge or sores or bumps on the genitals do not always point to an STD. People can get infections that cause such symptoms even if they have never had sex. Bumps on the genitals might turn out to be just pimples. A discharge from the vagina may occur quite normally at certain times in a girl's or woman's monthly cycle. A doctor can tell whether these kinds of problems are really anything to worry about.[5]

2

Hijacking the Reproductive System

IN THE SEVENTEENTH CENTURY, a Dutchman, Anton van Leeuwenhoek, spent much of his spare time on his hobby. He made microscopes and used them to look at things. He was so good at his craft that his microscopes were better than the ones scientists were using at the time. His was just a simple microscope with a single lens, but it could magnify an object up to two hundred times. Leeuwenhoek was not a doctor or a scientist. He actually sold cloth for a living. But it wasn't long before he realized that building microscopes could be more than just a hobby.

Although he did not receive a higher education or university degrees in science, Leeuwenhoek was a smart, curious man. He collected a variety of things to look at under the microscope, including water, plants, blood, and dirt. He even took a sample of scrapings from the film on his own teeth. In that sample, he made an exciting discovery: He saw living creatures he called animalcules ("little animals"). This was the first time anyone had ever seen what we now call bacteria.[1]

What Are Bacteria?

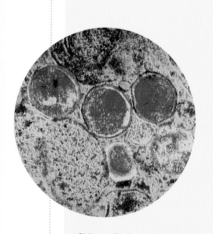

Chlamydia bacteria (falsely colored pink) inside a cell.

Bacteria are tiny living organisms made up of only one cell. Under a microscope, they can be seen in different shapes and sizes. Some are shaped like little balls, others like tiny rods, and still others like wiggly corkscrews.

Some bacteria can live on their own, in ponds or soil. Others must depend on another organism (their host) for survival. Some bacteria harm their host, stealing nutrients and producing poisons. The harmful bacteria we call "germs" can cause diseases. Under the right conditions, bacteria can multiply very quickly. A bacterium can reproduce in just twenty minutes. That means that a single bacterium could grow and divide into millions of bacteria in seven hours. While the body is defending itself against these intruders, we may feel miserable.

Anton van Leeuwenhoek discovered that microscopic creatures, such as those that cause STDs, live in the human body. Here he shows off his microscope to Catherine of England.

Leeuwenhoek's discovery uncovered a whole new world: Microscopic creatures were living inside our own bodies! These creatures, which can be seen only with a microscope, are called microorganisms. Microorganisms can live just about anywhere, especially in places that are warm and moist. The nooks and crannies of the human body supply everything a living creature could need—food, shelter, and a cozy place to reproduce.

"Good" Germs?

Bacteria are often considered "bad" or "harmful." It is true that some bacteria are germs that can make people very sick. But most bacteria do not harm us at all—in fact, some of them help us. Millions and millions of bacteria live inside our intestines. These bacteria help destroy other organisms that could be harmful. Some break food down to make it easier to digest. Others make important vitamins that make us healthy and strong.

The skin in the genital area—around the reproductive organs and in the linings of the body openings—are particularly good habitats for many different kinds of tiny creatures. These parts of the body are usually covered, which helps to keep them warm, moist, and mostly undisturbed—perfect conditions for bacterial growth and survival. Moreover, the way humans reproduce provides a way for our uninvited "guests" to spread from one host to another. To understand exactly how the organisms that cause STDs can live and spread, we need some background on the human reproductive organs and the things people do when they are "having sex."

The Male Parts

Most of the male sex organs are on the outside of the body. Males have two main sex organs—the penis and the testicles.

The penis is a tube-shaped organ that allows sperm—the male sex cells—to be transferred to the female. The testicles, or testes, are two egg-shaped structures that hang behind the penis. They are protected by a loose bag of skin called the scrotum. When a boy matures, parts of his body begin to change. The testes start to produce sperm. During sexual activity, the sperm travel to the penis through a passageway called the seminal duct. Before leaving the body, sperm are mixed with fluids to form a milky white

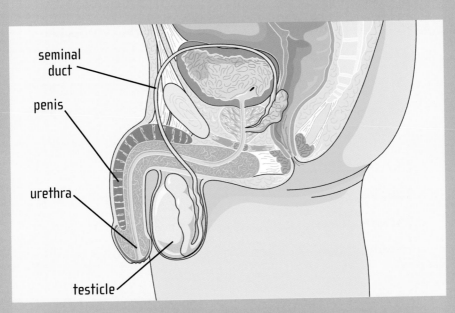

The male reproductive organs.

liquid called semen. The semen carries the sperm out of the body through the urethra. Humans also urinate through the urethra, but urine and semen never go through the urethra at the same time. The passage of semen out of the penis is called ejaculation.

The Female Parts

Most of the female sex organs are on the *inside* of the body. The vagina is a stretchy, moist passageway that leads to the reproductive organs inside. Its entrance is located below the opening of the urethra. (There is no connection between the vagina and the urethra.) Glands in the vagina produce fluid that keeps the area moist.

The vagina leads to the cervix, the entrance to the uterus. The uterus, or womb, is shaped like an upside-down pear. One oval-shaped ovary lies on each side of the uterus. The sides of the uterus extend out into two fallopian tubes. These tubes curve over each side, with their open ends close to the ovaries. The ovaries contain the female sex cells, called eggs. Each month, an egg is released from one of the ovaries and travels through the closest fallopian tube into the uterus. This process is called ovulation. After ovulation, the lining of the

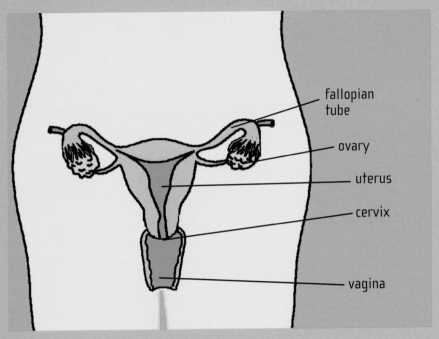

The female reproductive organs.

uterus gets even thicker. It fills with blood and nutrients to support the egg in case it joins with a sperm. If this joining, called fertilization, happens, the woman becomes pregnant. A fetus will then grow in the uterus.

If the egg is not fertilized, it shrivels up. The thick lining of the uterus starts to break apart. After a while, blood and tissue from the lining pass out through the vagina. The blood flow is called menstruation, or a period. This monthly cycle, called the menstrual cycle, happens about every 28 days.

It's Normal to Bleed!

A girl or woman who is menstruating is not sick. She is in no danger of bleeding to death. Menstruation is a normal body process. It gets rid of the extra material from the lining of the uterus when it is not needed for nourishing a growing baby. The blood vessels in the lining clamp together and stop the bleeding as bits of the lining detach. While it might look as if a lot of blood is lost during menstruation, it actually involves only a few tablespoons.

How STDs Happen

STDs can spread when germs are transferred from one person to another during sexual intercourse or any skin-to-skin contact of the genitals. For example, germs that live and grow in semen or in the lining of a male's urethra may be transferred to a female during sexual intercourse. If the female's vagina contains germs, they may be transferred to the male. In other kinds of sexual activity, germs can pass from one partner's sex organs to the mouth during oral sex, or through the anus of the partner during anal sex. STDs that people can catch in these ways include syphilis, chlamydia, gonorrhea, herpes, and AIDS.

Despite their name, sexually transmitted diseases can also be passed from one person to another in ways that do not involve sex. For example, a pregnant woman with an STD may give the infection to her unborn child. Drug addicts may accidentally transfer blood if they share needles to "shoot up." Some of the blood from one person remains in the needle and may be injected into the next person who uses it. Drug users have an increased risk for developing hepatitis or AIDS.

STDs are passed from one person to another during sexual activity.

Same-Sex Partners

Sex between a male and a female isn't the only kind of sexual relationship. People who are sexually attracted to those of the opposite sex are called heterosexuals. Those who are attracted to people of the same sex are called homosexuals. STDs can be passed between homosexuals during oral or anal sex.

Many people think that gay women cannot get STDs, but that is not true. Some infections, such as herpes, syphilis, and genital warts, can be spread simply by skin-to-skin contact with the genitals. Sexual intercourse is not needed for transmission.

Who Gets STDs?

Anybody who is sexually active is at risk for getting a sexually transmitted disease. It can happen to people who have had sex fifty times or to those who are having sex for the first time. It takes only one person with an STD to spread the disease. However, the more sex partners a person has, the greater the risk of getting an STD. In addition, someone who has an STD is more likely to get another one. But anyone who is in a monogamous relationship—each having sex with just the other person—will *not* get an STD, as long as both partners do not have an STD.

In heterosexual relationships, women have a greater risk than men of getting an STD. For one thing, it is easier for germs to enter a woman's body during sexual intercourse. During sex, a man sends his semen, which may contain harmful organisms, directly into the woman's body. There it is warm and moist, the perfect breeding ground for germs. But most of the woman's body fluids remain on the outside of the man's penis and on the surrounding area, and germs are less likely to get inside.

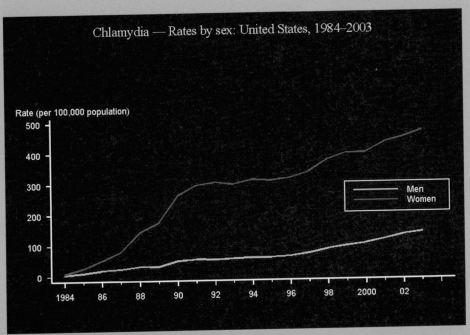

Women have a higher risk of getting an STD than men do. This graph shows how much higher the rate of chlamydia infection is in women than in men.

STDs can also be a bigger problem for women. Women are less likely than men to have noticeable symptoms. They may not get the treatment they need. This gives the disease a better chance to spread and become more serious. Men, on the other hand, often do have symptoms and are more likely to get them treated sooner. Women may be infected with an STD much longer than men, especially with such diseases as gonorrhea and chlamydia.

3

Syphilis

JEFFREY WAS IN HIS SOPHOMORE YEAR of college. While studying for his midterm exams, he was having a hard time concentrating. He was feeling tired and sort of sick—as though he was coming down with something. For the previous few days, he had also been noticing a strange rash. Reddish bumps had appeared first on his face. He thought it was just acne. But then the bumps started appearing on his back and chest, and he also had a few on his arms and legs. He thought it might be chickenpox, but the bumps didn't itch. Besides, he had already had chickenpox when he was a kid.

Finally Jeffrey decided to go to the student health center. There the doctor examined his rash and asked

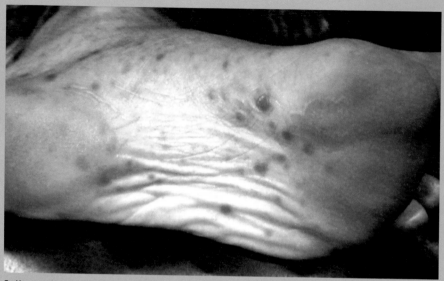

College student Jeffrey noticed a rash on his body, similar to the one shown here. He was diagnosed with syphilis. A person with syphilis may break out in a rash after weeks or months with no symptoms.

him some questions. Jeffrey wondered why he was being asked about whether he was sexually active and whether he had noticed any sores on his penis. He told the doctor that he had been with a few girls the last couple of months. Thinking back, he remembered that he had noticed a sore on his penis over a month ago. It didn't hurt, and it went away after a few days, so he didn't pay much attention to it. While talking to the doctor, Jeffrey recalled that the sore had appeared a little over a week after a big frat party where he had had sex with a girl he met there. They had both been doing some drinking. "I'll know more after the blood test results come back," the doctor said, "but it looks like you may have syphilis."

The blood test for syphilis was positive. The doctor gave Jeffrey a shot of penicillin and made an appointment for a follow-up visit. Meanwhile, the doctor asked Jeffrey about the girls he had been with since he had become infected. There was a good chance he might have transmitted the disease to them. They would need to be contacted to come in for a test.

Most of the rash disappeared within ten days after Jeffrey was treated. A follow-up blood test showed no traces of syphilis. Jeffrey was told it was a good thing the infection was caught early, before the bacteria had a chance to cause serious damage. But he was advised that he could catch syphilis again unless he protected himself.[1]

Many people think of syphilis as a thing of the past. Nobody gets *that* anymore, they think. But the disease has not yet disappeared. Indeed, the number of syphilis cases reported in the United States has gone down dramatically over the years—from 94,957 in 1946 to 5,979 in 2000. Since the numbers have been so low, the surgeon general announced a plan in 1999 to eliminate syphilis in America. However, the number of syphilis infections had a slight increase in 2001, with reports of 6,103 cases, and further increases in 2002 (6,862 cases)

What's In a Name?

The common name for syphilis used to be "the great pox"—
"great" because of its devastating effects across Europe and
"pox" because of the sores on the skin that are typical signs of
the disease. (Later, smallpox got its name to distinguish it from
great pox.) The medical name, syphilis, comes from a poem
written in 1530 by a physician and poet, Girolamo Fracastoro. The
poem was about Syphilus, a shepherd who was infected with the
great pox.

A shepherd once (distrust not ancient fame)
Possest these Downs, and Syphilus his Name;
Some destin'd Head t'attone the Crimes of all,
On Syphilus the dreadful Lot did fall.
Through what adventures this unknown Disease
So lately did astonisht Europe seize,
Through Asian coasts and Libyan Cities ran,
And from what Seeds the Malady began,
Our Song shall tell: to Naples first it came
From France, and justly took from France his Name . . .

—Girolamo Fracastoro, 1530
(translated from Latin by Nahum Tate)

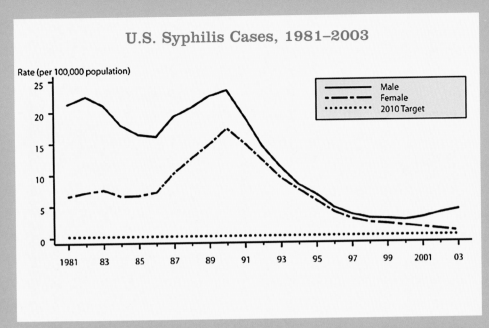

U.S. Syphilis Cases, 1981–2003

This graph shows the total number of syphilis cases from 1981 to 2003 in both males (solid line) and females (dashed line). The dotted line represents the target for the lower number of cases in 2010.

and 2003 (7,177 cases).[2] Health experts believe that these numbers may not tell the whole story. Many cases are not detected or reported. It is estimated that as many as 70,000 new syphilis cases may occur in the United States each year. Worldwide, there are an estimated 12 million new cases of syphilis each year.[3]

What Is Syphilis?

Syphilis is caused by a spiral-shaped bacterium called *Treponema pallidum.* This kind of bacterium is known as a spirochete, and it can live anywhere in the body.

All in the Family

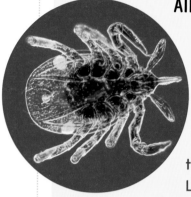

A magnified image of a deer tick.

You've probably heard of a disease caused by another member of the spirochete family: Lyme disease. This is caused by a spirochete called *Borrelia burgdorferi*. This spirochete lives inside the guts of ticks. The disease is passed to people through the bite of an infected tick. The signs of Lyme disease are similar to those of syphilis. In Lyme disease, a characteristic rash appears and can spread very quickly. Flulike symptoms may also appear. And like syphilis, the rash and other symptoms may come and go. Lyme disease spirochetes can also enter the bloodstream and spread to other parts of the body. If the disease is not treated, serious problems involving the heart or nervous system may develop.

Syphilis can be transmitted during sexual intercourse (vaginal, anal, or oral sex) and by kissing. Pregnant women with the disease can pass it to their unborn child. People *cannot* get syphilis from contact with toilet seats, doorknobs, clothes, or eating utensils. Spirochetes need moisture to survive. They quickly dry out and die when they are exposed to air.

What Are the Symptoms?

When syphilis is left untreated, the condition will go through four different phases, each with its own set of symptoms:

1. First stage (lasting up to six weeks): Symptoms usually develop about three weeks after infection. The first sign of the disease is a sore called a chancre. It appears on the vagina, penis, rectum, lips, or mouth. Syphilis chancres are small and do not itch or hurt, so they might not be noticed. However, a chancre is full of syphilis bacteria, which can easily spread to other people. The chancres disappear after a few weeks, but the bacteria are not gone. They enter the bloodstream and travel to other parts of the body.

2. Second stage (lasting up to a year): After a couple of weeks or months with no symptoms, the infected person may break out in a rash, which may appear anywhere on the body. The rash does not itch. Flulike symptoms may also develop, including fever, headache, sore throat, swollen lymph glands, muscle aches, and feelings of fatigue (extreme tiredness). People who do not get a rash might still go untreated. During the second stage, symptoms may disappear and then return.

3. Latent stage (lasting months or years): The third phase is a kind of "silent" stage. During this time, there are no symptoms of the disease. It looks as if the disease is gone, but the spirochetes are still lurking in the body.

Treponema pallidum bacterium that causes syphilis

What Causes the Symptoms?

When syphilis bacteria invade the body, they damage skin cells. The injured cells send out chemical alarm signals to call for help. These chemicals cause the walls of the tiny blood vessels in the skin to widen and leak. Fluid from the blood seeps out into the tissues, which causes the skin to become inflamed—swollen, hot, and red. Inflammation can make a person uncomfortable; but it allows white blood cells, the body's defenders, to move freely into infected tissues to battle the invading germs. "Swollen glands" are actually lymph nodes in which white blood cells gather and wage furious battles against germs traveling in the body fluids. Fever and headache are other results of the body's efforts to defend itself.

4. Third (or late) stage: When the syphilis bacteria finally come out of hiding, they may attack the heart, brain, bones, liver, or any other organ in the body. In the late stage, serious damage is done to the body. Health problems include paralysis (inability to move limbs), numbness, gradual blindness, and mental illness. Severe damage may result in death. Fortunately, most syphilis cases—about 70 percent—do not reach the third stage, because patients seek medical treatment before it is too late.[4]

Detecting and Treating Syphilis

It is important to catch syphilis early, while the germs are still easy to kill and before the disease has a chance to cause too much damage. One way to test for syphilis is by taking material from a chancre or rash and examining it under a powerful microscope. The technician will look for syphilis bacteria. Sometimes it is not easy to see the bacteria, even if the person does have syphilis.

Syphilis can be detected by looking at a chancre or rash sample under the microscope.

There are also several kinds of blood tests for syphilis. The tests use chemicals to detect antibodies made by a person's immune system. Antibodies are proteins that match a particular germ or foreign chemical. A person who has syphilis will have antibodies against syphilis bacteria. The test is usually accurate, but not 100 percent. It can take up to six weeks to build up enough antibodies in the blood to be detected by a blood test. During this time, a blood test may be negative, even though the person has been infected.

The best treatment for syphilis is penicillin. A large dose of penicillin is injected into a muscle. Only one

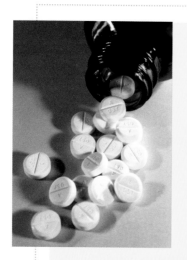

Still Good After All These Years

Penicillin has been used to treat syphilis since the 1950s. Some diseases have become drug resistant to certain antibiotics, including penicillin. That means that the bacteria have somehow changed and can no longer be killed by one or more types of antibiotics. Fortunately, syphilis is not one of them. Even with all the new drugs available, penicillin is still the best way to treat syphilis.

shot is needed if the person was infected within the previous year. For people who are allergic to penicillin, other antibiotics can be used. For some people, penicillin treatment may have unpleasant side effects,

It is important to catch syphilis early, while the germs are still easy to kill and before the disease has a chance to cause too much damage.

including fever, headaches, sweating, and chills, and the chancres or rash may suddenly get worse. These symptoms are only temporary. They are the result of the body's reaction to the spirochetes killed by the drug, and they go away within twenty-four hours. People who are treated for syphilis still need to get blood tests over the next few months to make sure that all of the syphilis bacteria have been killed.

4

Gonorrhea

SARAH LIVED IN A SMALL TOWN in Georgia. The daughter of a Baptist minister, Sarah had grown up in a household where they didn't talk much about any sexual matters. But at twenty-five years old, she was faced with the unthinkable—a sexually transmitted disease. Sarah hardly even knew what an STD was. Back in high school, she was considered a "nice girl." She didn't date much, and the furthest she went with a guy was a little kissing in the back of the gym. Her parents expected Sarah to be a virgin until marriage.

When Sarah attended the University of Georgia, she met Reggie, a funny, easygoing biochemistry major.

After a few months of dating, Sarah and Reggie started having sex, even though she was having doubts about what she was doing. Reggie didn't like using condoms. He convinced her that her birth control was enough protection. A few weeks after they started having sex, Sarah felt mild aches in her abdomen. She didn't pay too much attention to them at first. Soon the pains got worse, until Sarah collapsed in agony.

At the hospital emergency room, Sarah was told that she had an infection and was given antibiotics. Tests would be needed to find out what kind of infection she had. It took several days for the results to come back. Finally, her doctor told her that she had gonorrhea. Sarah had no idea what that was. A nurse had to come in with a book to show her what it was all about. Sarah couldn't believe she had gotten an STD. She thought that STDs were something that happened to other people, not to a "nice" girl like her. Antibiotics wiped out Sarah's infection.

Sarah could never tell her parents that she had gotten an STD. The one person she did have to tell was Reggie. He went to a clinic right away to get tested. The results came back negative, but he was put on antibiotics anyway, since it was probably a false negative. Sarah wondered about Reggie's sex life before she knew him. He could have picked up STD germs from anyone in his past. Despite this ordeal, Sarah decided to stay with Reggie. But now Sarah doesn't really care for sex anymore, which has put a strain on the relationship. The thought of getting another STD is just too frightening.[1]

What Is Gonorrhea?

Gonorrhea, sometimes called the clap, is caused by a bacterium called *Neisseria gonorrhoeae*. The bacterium was named after Albert Neisser, the physician who in 1879 discovered the cause of this disease. Gonorrhea is one of the most common STDs in the United States. In 2002, there were 351,852 new cases of gonorrhea reported. But the Centers for Disease Control and Prevention (CDC) believes that the number of new cases is actually much higher—as many as 700,000 cases—half of which go unnoticed or unreported.[2]

> Gonorrhea is one of the most common STDs in the United States.

Gonorrhea bacteria may infect the reproductive organs, eyes, throat, urethra (urine canal), and rectum in both men and women. The disease is transmitted through sexual contact (vaginal, oral, or anal). A pregnant woman can pass gonorrhea to her baby during the birth. Or a person can get an eye infection by touching his or her infected

> Like most other STDs, gonorrhea bacteria need a moist environment to survive, so people cannot "catch" the disease by touching a doorknob, dry towel, or toilet seat.

genitals (penis or vagina) and then touching the eyes. Like most other STDs, gonorrhea bacteria need a moist environment to survive, so people cannot "catch" the disease by touching a doorknob, dry towel, or toilet seat.

What Are the Symptoms?

Men are more likely than women to have symptoms. About 10 to 15 percent of infected men and up to 80 percent of infected women do not show any obvious symptoms until the disease becomes more serious.[3] When symptoms *do* develop, they usually appear about two to ten days after infection. In some rare cases, it can take up to thirty days for symptoms to appear.

In men, the infection usually develops first in the penis and urethra. The bacteria may also invade the blood vessels and spread to other parts of the body. This is a condition known as disseminated gonorrhea, which

41

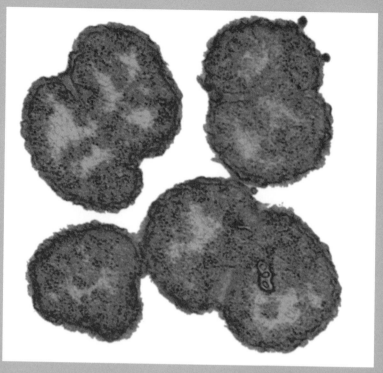

Neisseria gonorrhoeae bacteria are shown here with color enhancement and are magnified 100,000 times. These bacteria cause the STD known as gonorrhea.

causes a fever and a skin rash. If the bacteria spread to the knees, elbows, fingers, or other joints, a serious infection called septic arthritis may develop. The joints become swollen, stiff, and very painful to move.

In women, the cervix is the most common place for gonorrheal infection. However, the bacteria can spread to the uterus, fallopian tubes, and ovaries. This can lead to a more serious condition called pelvic inflammatory disease (PID). Damage to the infected areas may result in scarring. The condition may cause a fever and severe pain in the lower abdomen.

PID affects more than one million women in the United States. It should be treated as early as possible. Otherwise, serious health problems may develop. For as many as 10 percent of infected women, PID may result in infertility or an ectopic pregnancy.[4] An ectopic pregnancy occurs when a fertilized egg develops inside one of the fallopian tubes instead of in the uterus. This type of pregnancy is extremely dangerous and may be fatal for the mother, as well as for the fetus. (Men can also have fertility problems if the infection causes scarring in the urethra.)

Gonorrhea Symptom Checklist for Men

Gonorrhea may cause one or more of the following symptoms in men:

- A painful discharge of white, yellow, or green pus from the penis
- A frequent need to urinate
- Painful urination; there may be a burning sensation
- Swollen testicles

Gonorrhea Symptom Checklist for Women

Most women have mild symptoms or none at all. Those who do have one or more of the following:

- Urination becomes painful; may experience a burning sensation

- A yellowish or sometimes bloody discharge from the vagina

- Bleeding between menstrual periods

- Heavy bleeding during the menstrual period

- Pain during sexual intercourse

- Pain in the lower abdomen

Rectal gonorrhea (infection in the rectum or anus) may result from anal sex. It can affect both men and women. Symptoms include a discharge of thick fluid, itching, soreness, bleeding, and sometimes painful bowel movements. Oral sex with an infected person may lead to a throat infection. The throat may feel sore. Most of the time, however, infections of the throat or anus do not have noticeable symptoms.

Diagnosing and Treating Gonorrhea

Detecting gonorrhea is not always easy, especially if there are no obvious symptoms—but early detection is very important. It is a good idea for people who are sexually active to get tested for gonorrhea periodically, especially if they are involved with more than one partner.

Several tests can be used to diagnose gonorrhea. One test, called a Gram's stain, uses a sample of the discharge (fluid) from the penis or cervix. The sample is smeared on a slide and stained with a dye. This makes it easier to

Typically, patients with STDs are tested for gonorrhea and chlamydia at the same time, because these diseases have similar symptoms.

see any gonorrhea bacteria under a microscope. The Gram's stain gives quick results right in the doctor's office. The test results for women are not very accurate, so this test is rarely used for them.

A more reliable test is a gonorrhea culture. This test involves placing a sample of discharge on a laboratory dish. After about two days, the bacteria will have multiplied into millions, so they are easier to identify under a microscope. A culture is much more accurate than a Gram's stain, but it can take two days for the results to come back. Unfortunately, that gives the bacteria in the body more time to multiply and spread.

Another test for gonorrhea detects bacterial DNA in a sample of urine or discharge from the penis or cervix. (DNA is the chemical that contains instructions for inherited traits.) Health experts can identify organisms by their DNA. This test is much faster and even more accurate than the bacterial culture.

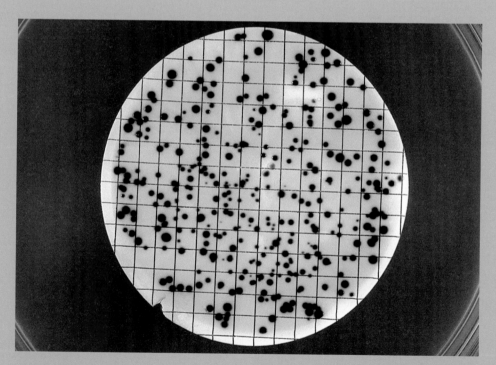

A gonorrhea culture shows the bacteria *Neisseria gonorrhoeae*, which causes gonorrhea. The sample was placed in this lab dish forty hours prior to this photo.

Doctors like to use more than one test to make an accurate diagnosis. Typically, patients with STDs are tested for gonorrhea and chlamydia at the same time, because these diseases have similar symptoms.

Since gonorrhea can lead to serious damage, treatment should begin as soon as possible. Gonorrhea can be treated effectively with antibiotics. Unlike syphilis, gonorrhea bacteria have become resistant to penicillin. When penicillin was first used to treat sexually transmitted diseases, it cured gonorrhea almost 100 percent of the time. Over time, the gonorrhea bacteria changed, and the new types (or strains) could no longer be killed by penicillin. These drug-resistant strains multiplied and spread. When doctors found out that penicillin no longer worked against gonorrhea, they tried another antibiotic, tetracycline. Eventually, the bacteria became resistant to this drug, too. Then scientists had to work hard to come up with new drugs to treat gonorrhea. Now there are a number of antibiotics that can be used to treat gonorrhea effectively. These antibiotics can be taken as an injection or in pill form.

A pregnant woman can pass chlamydia to her baby.

5

Chlamydia

MARIA HAD BEEN HAPPILY MARRIED for eight years and had just given birth to her third child. A few weeks later, her new baby got sick. He had been coughing for a few days, and the coughing kept getting worse. He became so congested, he could hardly breathe. The pediatrician diagnosed pneumonia and admitted the baby to the hospital. Laboratory tests showed that the baby's pneumonia was caused by chlamydia. It was the same kind of chlamydia that is transmitted sexually! Maria was shocked. "Where did he get it?" The doctor suspected that the baby had gotten the disease from Maria, so he tested her. The test showed that she had chlamydia as well. Maria couldn't believe it. She had never had any symptoms, and she had been faithful to her husband throughout the marriage. She wondered if her husband had been cheating on her.

Maria's husband assured her that he had been faithful, too, but his test was also positive for chlamydia. The doctor explained that chlamydia can hide in a person's body for many years, without showing any symptoms. Either Maria or her husband could have become infected during a past relationship, before they ever met.

> Chlamydia is one of the most common sexually transmitted diseases.

Maria, her husband, and their baby were all treated with antibiotics. The baby recovered quickly and was soon well enough to go back home. Meanwhile, tests of the two older children came back negative. Apparently they were lucky and had not been infected during their births.[1]

What Is Chlamydia?

Chlamydia is caused by the bacterium *Chlamydia trachomatis*. It is one of the most common sexually transmitted diseases. An estimated 3 million Americans are infected with chlamydia each year. Many of them do not even know that they have been infected.[2] As a result, people can unknowingly pass the disease to others.

Like most other STDs, chlamydia is usually passed from one person to another during sexual contact (oral, vaginal, or anal). Newborns can catch the disease during the birth. The infected baby may get pneumonia or develop an eye infection. These days, in many hospitals around the country, newborns are routinely given medicated eyedrops to prevent an eye infection—just in case the mother is infected with gonorrhea or chlamydia.

When they find out they have chlamydia, many people, like Maria, worry that their partner has been unfaithful. But these bacteria may remain inside the body, without causing any trouble, for years. People can be infected in their teen years and live a normal life until one day, out of the blue, they find out they have chlamydia.

What Are the Symptoms?

Chlamydia is called the "silent disease" because most people don't show any symptoms. In fact, as many as 85 percent of women with chlamydia, and 40 percent of men, are without symptoms.[3] A disease without

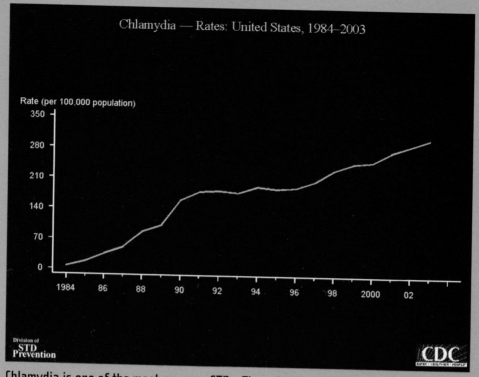

Chlamydia — Rates: United States, 1984–2003

Rate (per 100,000 population)

Chlamydia is one of the most common STDs. The rate of chlamydia infection has been increasing, as shown in this chart for the U.S. population, 1984-2003.

symptoms doesn't sound too bad. However, if left untreated, chlamydia, like gonorrhea, can lead to pelvic inflammatory disease (PID) in women. Remember that PID can cause severe damage to a woman's uterus, fallopian tubes, and/or ovaries, which may result in infertility or an ectopic pregnancy.

If symptoms *do* develop, they usually appear one to three weeks after the infection. Just as in gonorrhea, signs and symptoms for women may include an abnormal discharge from the vagina, pain when urinating, lower abdominal pain, fever, pain during intercourse, and bleeding between menstrual periods.

In men, signs and symptoms are also very similar to those of gonorrhea. They may include a discharge from the penis, pain or a burning feeling when urinating, and pain and swelling in the testicles.

Men or women who have anal sex can develop an infection in their rectum, which may cause pain and itching, discharge, or bleeding. Those who have oral sex can develop an infection in their throats, which may become sore. However, infections of the throat or rectum rarely produce symptoms.

Diagnosing and Treating Chlamydia

Generally, chlamydia is a greater concern for women than for men because of the risk of PID. However, early

A Common Link

Chlamydia and gonorrhea are two separate diseases, caused by two different bacteria. But they share the same symptoms, as well as complications. In fact, sometimes the two infections are confused for each other.

detection is very important for men as well. In men, the disease is less likely to cause serious damage, but infections can occur. Unless they are treated, men with chlamydia can become sterile (infertile). Also, even if they have no symptoms, infected men can still transmit the disease to women.

Laboratory tests of urine or of samples of material collected from the genital organs can be used to diagnose chlamydia. In 2003 British researchers announced that they had developed a new test for chlamydia, called Firstburst. This test is easy to use and can give results in less than twenty-five minutes. For men, a dipstick is used to test for bacteria in a urine sample. For women, the sample is taken from the vagina using a cotton swab. The urine test for men is not as accurate as the swab test for women, however.

Diagnostic tests are not 100 percent effective. It may take more than one test to give an accurate diagnosis. Some people may have both gonorrhea and chlamydia. In these cases, they need to be treated for both conditions. But the antibiotics that work for gonorrhea do not work for chlamydia, and vice versa. Penicillin will not work for either disease, but there are a number of effective alternatives.

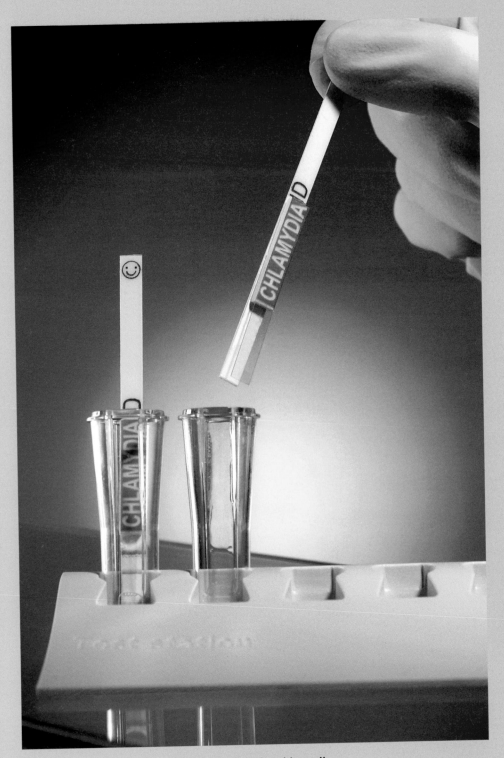

Firstburst test for chlamydia.

A few health experts recommend that people who are sexually active, especially those with more than one partner, be screened for chlamydia at least twice a year. Most recommend screening once a year for sexually active women twenty-five or younger. Older women who have a new sex partner or have sex with multiple partners should also have annual chlamydia tests.[4] This can help a great deal in detecting this "silent disease" before it causes trouble.

6

Herpes

CURTIS WAS HEARTBROKEN after his divorce. After a little more than a year of the single life, though, he was ready to settle down again. He wanted to find someone he could spend the rest of his life with. Dating the second time around wasn't easy. Curtis couldn't seem to find the right person. The search became even tougher when he found out that he had contracted genital herpes. Curtis was devastated. "I was having difficulty as it was. With herpes I thought it would be impossible. I thought I was unlovable, untouchable, undesirable."[1]

Curtis had frequent outbreaks of herpes—small blisters appeared on his penis and in his genital area.

By following their doctor's advice and a medication schedule, patients with herpes can keep their outbreaks under control and avoid infecting their partners.

They would last about a week or so and then fade away. By the time the last one disappeared, a new one would show up. Curtis was very frustrated. His outbreaks seemed constant—he was "clear" for only one week every month.

Curtis was afraid that if he told women about his herpes, they would never want to date him. But he knew he had to be up front about it. He didn't want to infect someone else. The first time he told someone, it didn't go very well. After that, he realized that he had to educate himself about the disease and accept his situation before he could have a successful relationship.

Curtis did finally meet the right person. He was honest with Karen, now his wife, from the start. She was very understanding and accepting. She even went with Curtis to support group meetings for people with STDs. It was there that Karen realized that even though she didn't want to get herpes herself, Curtis was the man that she wanted to be with for the rest of her life. They agreed that they would find a way to be together and learn how to live with herpes safely.

When Curtis met Karen, he was on medication for his herpes. He continues to take the drugs daily to keep the outbreaks under control and reduce the chances of infecting Karen. During a year of this drug routine, Curtis has not had a single herpes outbreak.[2]

What Is Herpes?

When people hear the word *herpes*, they tend to think "STD." But there are actually two kinds of herpes, both caused by the herpes simplex virus (HSV). Most people—as much as 80 percent of the U.S. population—are infected with the first type, HSV-1.[3] HSV-1 usually infects the lips, causing painful blisterlike

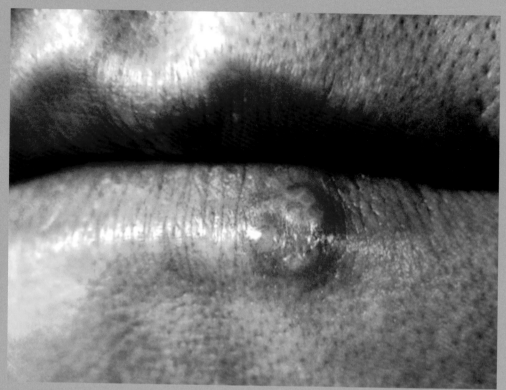

The HSV-1 virus causes sores on the lips. These are also called cold sores or fever blisters.

sores known as cold sores or fever blisters. HSV-2 causes genital herpes, producing sores in the genital area. Genital herpes is one of the most common STDs—an estimated 45 million Americans, ages twelve and older, are infected.[4]

People can get genital herpes by having sex (vaginal, anal, or oral) with someone who is having a herpes outbreak. An outbreak means that the virus is active. This is when the disease is most likely to be passed to another person. However, many people infected with the virus do not have any noticeable symptoms, so they could infect another person and not even know it.

Pregnant women with genital herpes can deliver a healthy baby. Mothers infected with the herpes virus before becoming pregnant have antibodies for herpes in their body. They can pass these protective antibodies to their newborn. However, herpes can be dangerous in pregnant women who become infected in the third trimester. There is not enough time to build up antibodies to protect the baby. The effects can be devastating. "More than 40 percent [of the babies] die or have severe brain damage," says Zane Brown, M.D., professor of obstetrics at the University of Washington in Seattle.[5]

Which Is It?

Someone who is infected with HSV-1 (cold sores) can give his or her partner an HSV-1 infection on the genitals by performing oral sex. The sores look just like those of HSV-2 genital herpes. And HSV-2, transmitted during oral sex, can cause an outbreak in the partner's mouth or throat. The symptoms look the same as ordinary cold sores; only laboratory tests can tell the difference.

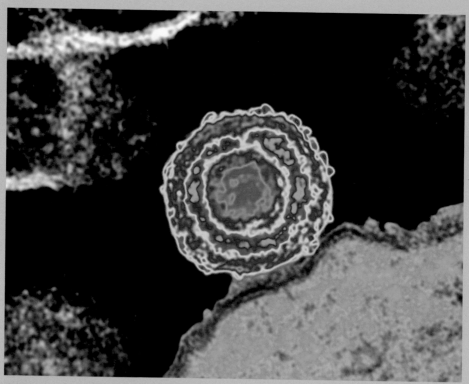

The herpes virus (multi-colored circle) is seen sitting on a cell (green-orange) and starting to enter it. This virus image was magnified 200 times and colored.

What Are the Symptoms?

When a person becomes infected with herpes, symptoms may develop within two to ten days. Depending on where the infection started, sores may appear in and around the vagina and on the cervix of women, and on the penis and scrotum on men. (A woman can't see sores on the cervix herself; a doctor uses special instruments to look deep inside the vagina.) In both men and women, sores may also develop around the anal opening, in the urinary passage, and on the buttocks, thighs, and hands. At first, small red bumps crop up, and soon develop into fluid-filled blisters, called vesicles. When these vesicles break open, they become painful, open sores. Within a week, the sores become crusty and then disappear without leaving any scars.

What Are Viruses?

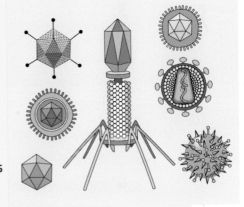

Viruses are the tiniest living organisms on Earth. They are smaller than bacteria. In fact, viruses cannot be seen through an ordinary microscope. Instead, a more powerful microscope, an electron microscope, is needed to see viruses. Some viruses look like balls with spikes sticking out all over. Others look like loaves of bread, coiled springs, or even tadpoles. Viruses depend on hosts to live, grow, and reproduce. They invade body cells and turn them into virus-making factories. When a cell is full of viruses, it bursts open, and hundreds of new viruses spill out. Each new virus finds another cell to invade, and continues the process. Soon there are millions of viruses in the body. While the body's defenses are attacking the intruders, the person may feel miserable.

After the first herpes outbreak goes away, the disease is not gone for good. Actually, it goes into hiding, and another outbreak may occur later on. Doctors call this a recurrence. What happens is that once the virus infects a person, it travels through the nerves and "hides out" at the end of the spine. During this time, the virus is inactive. It does not cause any harm. But later on, the

People can get genital herpes by having sex with someone who is having a herpes outbreak. An outbreak means that the virus is active.

virus may "wake up" and travel back through the nerves, until it reaches the skin surface, causing another herpes outbreak. Most people have four or five recurrences within the first year. After that, their outbreaks become less frequent and the symptoms become milder, usually lasting less than a week. However, people's symptoms vary greatly. Some people may only have one or two outbreaks during their whole life. Then there are people like Curtis, who may have outbreaks quite often.

Some people get warning signals that alert them of a recurrence. This is known as a prodrome. During a

Sign and Symptom Checklist

- Irritated red area or bumps may appear on genitals (penis or vagina), genital area, cervix, buttocks, around anal opening, thighs, or hands

- Fever

- Headache

- Muscle aches

- Itching or burning feeling in the genital or anal area, pain in the legs, buttocks, or genital area

- Feeling of pressure in the abdomen

- Uncomfortable or painful urination

- Vaginal discharge

- Swollen glands in the groin area

prodrome, a person may have a tingling or itching feeling in the genital area, or pain in the buttocks, down the legs, or in the lower back. Some people may get a prodrome, but they never develop any sores.

Scientists don't know exactly what causes herpes to come out of hiding. Some people insist their recurrences are triggered by stress, illness, poor nutrition, or menstruation. However, there is no solid evidence that this is true.

Detecting and Treating Herpes

Even though a doctor may recognize the sores as signs of genital herpes, a viral culture is usually needed to confirm the diagnosis. The doctor takes a sample of fluid from one of the vesicles. At the laboratory, the sample is mixed with a special solution that helps the viruses to multiply. The lab technician then analyzes the sample to see if any herpes viruses are present. This test can also show which kind of herpes simplex virus it

> There is no cure for herpes. Once a person is infected, the virus remains in the body for the rest of his or her life.

is, type 1 or type 2. It takes one to three days for the results to come back. If the test is positive, no other testing is needed. But if the test is negative, a blood test should be done. A blood test may also be used to diagnose herpes in a person who doesn't have any obvious symptoms but has had sex with someone who has herpes and is worried about a possible infection.

There is no cure for herpes. Once a person is infected, the virus remains in the body for the rest of his or her life. Antibiotics kill bacteria, but they will not work on viruses. Certain drugs, called antiviral drugs, can help ease the symptoms or shorten how long they last. These drugs can be taken at the first sign of an outbreak or every single day to keep the outbreaks from happening so often.

7

HIV and AIDS

CHERYL WAS FIFTEEN when she met Billy, a really hot-looking guy she had her eyes on in school. She heard that Billy was heavy into drugs, though. It couldn't be true, she thought. All she knew was that she wanted him to notice her. Then one day, he did. He flashed her a smile that drew her to him even more. Soon, they started to hang out together. He told her that she was beautiful and that she was the only one for him. This made her feel so good that she was determined to do anything she could to hold on to that feeling.

Cheryl decided to have sex with Billy. It was her first time. She wasn't sure if she should go through with it, but she didn't want to lose him. They didn't use a condom. Cheryl had gotten one from a friend, "just in case," but she was too afraid to mention it to Billy. What if it turned him off? What if it made him angry? What if he left because of it? She figured, "Maybe, just this once without protection won't matter." They did it only one time. She'd be fine, she hoped.

As it turned out, Billy ran away a few days later. He was deep into drugs, even sharing needles with the guy

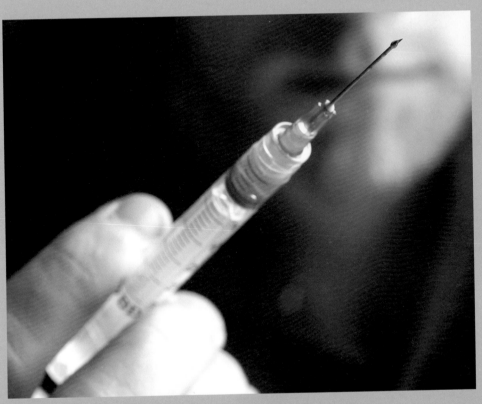

AIDS is a sexually transmitted disease. When needles are shared among drug users, the AIDS virus can also be passed from person to person.

who sold him the stuff. Now nobody knew where he was or what he was doing.

After Billy, Cheryl did not date much. She felt ashamed about what she had done. But seven years later, Cheryl got herself into a familiar situation. Again, she had unprotected sex with a guy. And again, she was too afraid to ask him to wear a condom. This time, she got pregnant.

A year after her daughter was born, Cheryl was not feeling like herself. She felt tired all the time. She had hardly any appetite, and she was losing a lot of weight. She went to the doctor's office to get checked out. They collected information from Cheryl about her symptoms and when they started; they also asked her about her sexual history. Then they took a blood sample. A few days later, test results showed that Cheryl had AIDS. Cheryl was in shock. That's impossible, she thought. She had had sex only twice in her entire life! Could her baby's father have infected her? Or . . . Billy, all those years ago? She had heard from friends that Billy was very sick now. And she knew he had been sharing needles with other drug addicts. But if it *was* Billy, then Cheryl had already been infected with HIV before she was pregnant. She hoped that her daughter would not develop AIDS, too. So far, tests showed that the baby was not infected. Cheryl couldn't take it if she had passed on this horrible disease to her child.[1]

What Is AIDS?

AIDS stands for *a*cquired *i*mmune *d*eficiency *s*yndrome. It is caused by a virus called HIV (*h*uman *i*mmunodeficiency *v*irus). HIV attacks the body by damaging or killing cells of the immune system. The immune system is our body's defense system. It includes several kinds of white blood cells, which protect us against invading germs. When the immune system is damaged by HIV, the body's defenses can no longer fight effectively against infections and cancer. The infections that affect people with AIDS are known as opportunistic infections. They are caused by viruses or bacteria that

Is It HIV or AIDS?

HIV is the name of the virus that causes AIDS. A person can be "HIV positive" (be infected with the virus) but not have the actual disease, AIDS, yet. It can take a long time—even years—before symptoms of AIDS develop.

normally do not cause trouble in healthy people. But they can be very dangerous in AIDS patients. Opportunistic infections that are often seen in people with AIDS include an unusual kind of pneumonia, tuberculosis, and various kinds of cancer.

People with another STD, such as syphilis, gonorrhea, genital herpes, or chlamydia, have a greater risk of contracting HIV from an infected person. A sore or rash in the genital area provides an easy entryway for the virus.

> People with another STD, such as syphilis, gonorrhea, genital herpes, or chlamydia, have a greater risk of contracting HIV from an infected person.

AIDS is the deadliest of all the STDs today. It affects people all over the world. In 2003, an estimated 37.8 million people worldwide were living with HIV/AIDS. Of those, 2.1 million were younger than fifteen. That same year, there were nearly 3 million deaths worldwide from AIDS-related illnesses, which included about 490,000 children under the age of fifteen. Two-thirds of the 37.8 million HIV/AIDS patients lived in sub-Saharan Africa, and another 20 percent lived in Asia and the Pacific. In the United States, an estimated 850,000 to 950,000 Americans were infected with HIV, a quarter of whom did not even know that they were infected.[2]

How Do People Get AIDS?

HIV is usually spread by having unprotected sex with an infected person, mainly through vaginal or anal sex. Like other germs that cause STDs, HIV is passed from the genital organs of one partner to the genitals or rectum of the other. Rare cases of transfer during oral sex have also occurred. The virus may be found in all the body fluids of an infected person, especially in the blood, semen, and secretions from the vagina. It can infect cells in the lining of the rectum or vagina, or pass directly into the bloodstream through a cut or sore. Many studies have repeatedly shown that HIV *cannot* be transmitted through casual contact, such as touching a doorknob or a toilet seat, or talking to an infected person.

HIV can be passed from an infected mother to her baby, during the birth, or later if she breastfeeds the infant. (Breast milk is another body fluid that can carry HIV.) The virus can spread through transfers of blood, as well. Now that reliable tests for HIV infection are available and blood donors are carefully screened, blood

"Soul Buddyz" characters from the book series

Reaching Out to the World's Teens

AIDS is a worldwide problem, and health experts all over the world are targeting teenagers with kid-friendly education efforts. In South Africa, for example, teens used to get very little information about sex. Parents did not want to give their children "bad ideas." The spread of AIDS began to change these views, but a poll reported in 2002 found that only 22 percent of teenagers had learned about sex from their parents. (Seventy percent said they wished they had.) Educators are trying to spread the word about safe sex through a popular TV and radio soap opera, *Soul City*, set in a township clinic. Each year, when a new series of episodes begins, a million comic books based on the series are inserted in daily newspapers around the nation. The show also produces a ninth-grade "life skills" textbook and "Soul Buddyz" books and tapes for eight- to twelve-year-olds that reach about two-thirds of those students. In rural areas, where it is difficult to get books and tapes, schools put on annual plays about AIDS.[3]

transfusions do not pose much risk in the United States and other developed nations. In some poorer areas of the world, needles for transfusions or injections of drugs are reused without proper disinfection, and the disease may be spread in this way. Drug addicts who share needles can also be infected with HIV, and they may then transmit it to their sex partners.

What Are the Symptoms?

Many people do not develop any symptoms when they first become infected with HIV. Others may come down with a flulike illness after a month or two. The symptoms include fever, headache, tiredness, and swollen lymph nodes; these usually go away within a week or so. This early stage of HIV infection is often confused with other viral infections, such as a bad cold or flu. The person is very contagious during this time, and the genital fluids contain large amounts of virus.

Then, for up to ten years or more, there are no apparent symptoms. The infected person may not even know that he or she is infected. During this time, the person can still pass the virus to others. The virus is very much alive, multiplying, infecting, and killing cells of the host's immune system.

As the HIV infection progresses, or gets worse, other symptoms start to develop. The lymph nodes become swollen, because the body is battling the multiplying virus. Loss of appetite, weight loss, fever, rashes, night sweats, and fatigue are other typical symptoms of AIDS. The person may also develop memory loss, confusion, and various other mental problems if the brain has been infected by the virus. As the immune system weakens, opportunistic infections may develop. The symptoms that appear then are signs of AIDS-related illnesses. For example, coughing and shortness of breath are symptoms of pneumonia. The purplish spots on the skin of some people with AIDS are signs of a cancer called Kaposi's sarcoma.

> The term *AIDS* is used to describe the advanced stages of the HIV infection.

Diagnosing and Treating AIDS

The term *AIDS* is used to describe the advanced stages of the HIV infection. The CDC has developed certain guidelines to distinguish AIDS from HIV. First, AIDS is diagnosed in people infected with HIV who have a count of less than 200 helper T cells (a kind of white blood cell) per cubic millimeter of blood. Healthy people usually have a helper T cell count of 1,000 or more. In addition, an AIDS diagnosis depends on whether the person has developed any of twenty-six conditions, most of which are opportunistic infections.

Many people don't even think about getting themselves tested for HIV—unless they know that they have been exposed to the virus. Some people find out that

> There is no cure for AIDS, but researchers have developed a number of drugs for treating it.

they have been infected when they have routine tests done—to qualify for an insurance policy or a job, for example, or during a yearly gynecological visit.

Laboratory tests can detect HIV infection. In the most widely used tests, a sample of blood or saliva is tested for antibodies to HIV, not for the actual virus. It can take up to six months after the infection for the body to produce enough antibodies to show up in blood or saliva tests. Tests for HIV genes can detect infection

Daphne Rivera

SPOTLIGHT

Helping AIDS Patients All Over the World

José Clemente lives and works in Mexico. When he was diagnosed with HIV in 1994, José had no idea how he could afford all the drugs he would need to treat the disease. And without drugs, he would never have a fighting chance. But now, José *does* have a chance, thanks to Daphne Rivera, a health educator from Brooklyn, New York.

Daphne has been infected with HIV since 1992. She has been giving away her extra pills through the Aid to AIDS program since 1996. The drugs that are donated in the program are actually leftovers—after switching medicines, or taking a "drug holiday" as directed by the doctor. Some are donated from family and friends of patients who have died. Daphne

earlier. They are useful for determining how much virus is present in the blood. This information helps doctors decide whether an infected person is likely to develop AIDS. These tests can also help doctors follow how well treatment is working.

There is no cure for AIDS, but researchers have developed a number of drugs for treating it. Doctors have discovered that a combination of several drugs, finds the program very rewarding, "It's easy to give away pills you aren't using. But for the person getting them, it's really life or death."[4]

In 2004, it had been four years since José had started receiving medications from Daphne Rivera's supply. Even though they had never met, José was very grateful to Daphne for giving him more time to do all the things he always wanted to do.

In the United States, it is illegal to give away leftover pills to U.S. patients. Health officials are not allowed to deal with medication remaining from patients' prescriptions because of the risk of tampering. But they are allowed to donate the medicine to nonprofit groups to be shipped out of the country as aid. Most of the medications Aid for AIDS receives are not opened, and health care workers check those that have been opened before they ship them out. According to the World Health Organization, there have been no reports of secondhand AIDS drugs harming any patients.

which work in different ways, can kill enough viruses to bring the HIV infection under control. These drugs can be used not only for patients with active symptoms of AIDS but also for HIV-infected people who have not yet developed any symptoms. Their "viral load" (the amount of HIV in their bodies) may still be small enough that the infection can be wiped out, preventing them from developing AIDS in the future. Doctors who treat AIDS patients also have a number of drugs for treating opportunistic infections.

The most effective combinations of antiviral drugs cannot kill *all* of the AIDS viruses in a patient's body. Even when lab tests no longer show any traces of HIV, some viruses are still hiding out in the nerves or other tissues. This happens because antiviral drugs generally work only on viruses that are active. If the drug

> AIDS medications are not perfect. They can have some annoying and even life-threatening side effects.

treatments are stopped and then the person gets some other infection, the immune system goes into action. Then some of the hidden viruses "wake up" and start infecting white blood cells—and the disease starts all over again.

Many people are no longer as afraid of AIDS as they were when it first appeared. Knowing that they can protect themselves from infection—and that they cannot get AIDS through casual contact—has reduced their fears. Health experts believe, however, that some people may now be taking AIDS too lightly. They may have unprotected sex, figuring that they can just take medicine to treat the disease if they get it. But AIDS medications are not perfect. They can have some annoying and even life-threatening side effects, from nausea and diarrhea to a dangerous drop in the number of red or white blood cells, inflammation of the pancreas, and painful nerve damage. And the drugs must be taken for a long time, perhaps even for life.

8

Other STDs

SARA HAD HAD SEX with a couple of guys during her college years. Shortly after she graduated, at twenty-one years old, she noticed some strange-looking bumps on her vagina. She figured that they would just go away on their own, but instead, more of them appeared, and they were getting bigger. Finally, Sara went to her gynecologist, and she was diagnosed with genital warts, a kind of STD. Like many people, Sara never thought about the risks of sex other than unexpected pregnancy. What she found out was, STDs can happen to *anyone*.[1]

As mentioned in the first chapter, there are more than twenty-five kinds of STDs. So far we have described five of them in detail. This chapter will briefly discuss some of the other STDs that are out there.

Genital Warts

Genital warts are very common, affecting roughly 20 million people in the United States.[2] They are caused by a group of viruses called human papillomaviruses (HPV). There are more than a hundred different kinds of HPV, although not all of them infect humans. Some kinds of HPV cause the warts that appear on our hands or feet. You can "catch" warts by skin-to-skin contact

There are more than twenty-five kinds of sexually transmitted diseases.

with someone infected with the virus. Genital warts are also transmitted through skin-to-skin contact, during sexual activity with an infected partner.

Genital warts look a lot like the ones that people get on their hands or feet. They are small, pink bumps, which may be raised or flat. They don't hurt, but they may itch. The warts may start to look like little cauliflowers as they grow bigger. In many cases, though, the warts are so tiny that they can be seen only with a magnifying glass. Most people don't even know that they are infected with HPV. There may be no signs or symptoms. The virus can hide in the body, and it can take a few weeks, months, or even years for symptoms to appear. When warts do appear, they may show up in the genital areas of women and men (vagina, vulva, cervix; penis, scrotum), the anus, and sometimes the thighs.

A doctor usually diagnoses genital warts by looking at them. Sometimes he or she may need to put a special solution on the infected area. This makes the warts appear white and more noticeable. Some kinds of HPV may not produce visible warts, but may lead to a much more serious problem: cancer of the cervix. Fortunately, the abnormal cells that can develop into cancer can be detected by a routine pap test during a gynecological visit. Other types of HPV may cause cancer in the vulva, anus, or penis.

There is no cure for genital warts. The virus will stay in the body for a lifetime. In many cases, the warts will disappear on their own, but new ones appear later. Sometimes the warts won't go away, but they can be removed. The doctor may prescribe special creams, or certain procedures can be done to remove the warts, such as freezing (cryosurgery), burning, or laser treatment. If a wart is really large, surgery may be needed to remove it.

Hepatitis B

Hepatitis is an inflammation of the liver. It can lead to scarring of the liver, liver cancer, liver failure, and even death. It is usually caused by a virus, but it can also develop as a result of long-term use of alcohol or drugs. There are six different kinds of viral hepatitis, each of

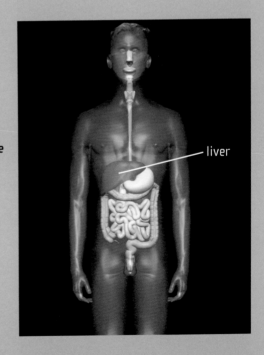

The liver is part of the digestive system. Hepatitis is an inflammation of the liver. Hepatitis B is an STD.

liver

which is caused by a different virus. The different kinds of hepatitis viruses are identified by the first six letters of the alphabet—A, B, C, D, E, and F. Although a couple of them may also be transmitted sexually, hepatitis B is the only one that is truly an STD.

Every year, about 300,000 Americans are infected with hepatitis B. And each year, about 5,000 people die from the disease.[3] The hepatitis B virus (HBV) can live in all body fluids, including blood, saliva, semen, and vaginal fluids. It can enter the body through cuts or tears in the skin, and through mucous membranes of

The hepatitis B virus can be transmitted through unprotected sex with an infected partner or by sharing infected needles.

the mouth, vagina, anus, and eyes. Hepatitis B is spread in the same ways as AIDS, but it is one hundred times more contagious. The hepatitis B virus can be transmitted through unprotected sex with an infected partner or by sharing infected needles. An infected mother may give it to her child during birth. Like HIV, hepatitis B infection can also be transmitted during contact sports (when there is a bleeding injury), by helping someone who is injured and bleeding, by sharing razors or toothbrushes, or by getting a tattoo or body piercing using infected instruments or needles.

In most cases (90 to 95 percent), hepatitis B does not cause any serious problems. The body is able to fight off the infection within a few months. Blood tests will show antibodies for HBV, even after the virus is gone. Anyone who is still infected after six months is considered a carrier. A carrier can transmit the disease to another person even though he or she doesn't show any symptoms. Unfortunately, as many as half of those infected with hepatitis don't even know that they have the disease, so they can unknowingly pass it to someone else. Some carriers may develop chronic hepatitis B. Their bodies are unable to bring the infection completely under control, and damage to the liver continues to worsen. Scar tissue gradually replaces normal tissue, blocking the flow of blood. Scarring may eventually affect so much of the liver that the organ can no longer do its work.

When symptoms *do* develop, they may appear up to six months after infection, although two to three months is average. Early signs of hepatitis may include flulike symptoms such as fatigue, low-grade fever, headache, loss of appetite, nausea, vomiting, and stiff or aching joints. The urine may become dark brown and foamy, and the feces may be pale. The person may develop jaundice, a condition in which the skin and whites of the eyes turn yellowish. There may also be pain in the abdomen.

There is no cure for hepatitis. Doctors usually recommend that patients get plenty of bed rest, lots of

Early signs of hepatitis may include flulike symptoms such as fatigue, low-grade fever, headache, loss of appetite, nausea, vomiting, and stiff or aching joints.

fluids, a healthy diet, and stay away from alcoholic drinks, which can damage the liver even further. For chronic hepatitis, the doctor may prescribe medication. Medications do not kill the hepatitis B virus, but they stop it from multiplying. This allows the liver to heal more quickly.

Can't Live Without It

The liver is the largest internal organ in the body, and a person can't live without it. It is found in the upper right side of the abdomen, in front of the stomach.

The liver has more than five hundred important jobs. It is the body's poison control center, removing poisons from the blood and changing them into harmless substances. It helps the body to digest fats; and it stores vitamins, minerals, and other food chemicals for later use. It makes a number of important proteins, including some that help the body fight infection. Proteins made by the liver also help to control growth and development.

The liver can take a lot of abuse. It will continue to work after as much as two-thirds of it is damaged. It can even grow back to normal size if up 70 percent is removed. But when the liver becomes too damaged to function, a person will die.

Trichomoniasis

Trichomoniasis, sometimes called trich, is caused by the protozoan *Trichomonas vaginalis*. This tiny one-celled organism thrives in the warm, moist environment of the human body. It can be passed from one person to another through sexual intercourse. Unlike most other STDs, it can survive a few hours on damp towels, wash-cloths, and bathing suits. Therefore, the disease can also

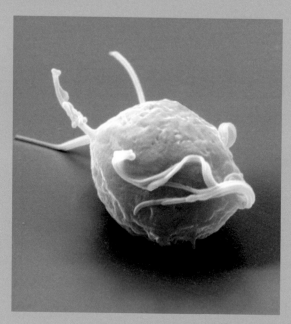

The *Trichomonas vaginalis* protozoan, a single-celled organism, causes the STD trichomoniasis. This image is magnified 9,000 times.

spread to a person who uses any of these items or puts on a bathing suit worn by an infected person without washing it first. A pregnant woman who is infected can also transmit the disease to her baby during delivery. Trichomoniasis is a common STD, affecting more than seven million Americans every year.[4]

Like many STDs, trichomoniasis often goes unnoticed. Most people do not show any symptoms. As you now know, that's how STDs are often spread—by people who do not even know they are infected. In some people, symptoms may appear five to twenty-eight days after exposure, although sometimes it can take months or longer. In women, the vagina is the target area. Symptoms may include a painful inflammation of the vagina; a yellowish, smelly discharge from the vagina; itchiness in the vagina; pain during urination; and feeling uncomfortable during sex. In men, the urethra is the target area. While rare, symptoms may include some irritation inside the penis, mild discharge, or slight burning after urination or ejaculation.

Trichomoniasis can be detected through a physical exam and laboratory tests. In women, a pelvic exam can show small, red sores on the vaginal wall or cervix caused by the infection. However, laboratory tests are more reliable. In men and women, samples of discharge can be cultured for the organism. Unfortunately, this can take up to two weeks. Some doctors may take a sample and look at it in their office. If they spot the protozoan, the infection can be treated with an antibiotic. As with other curable STDs, it is a good idea to treat both partners with antibiotics, even if only one of them has symptoms.

Pubic Lice (Crabs)

Pubic lice are commonly called crabs because they look like little crabs under a really strong magnifying glass. They are actually tiny insects that can attach themselves

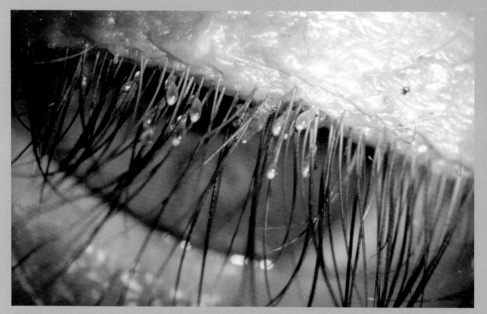

Pubic lice can live on pubic hair, or even the hair on legs and armpits. They are also found on mustaches, beards, eyebrows, or eyelashes, as shown here.

with their clamplike claws to pubic hair in the genital area. Sometimes they can even be found on the hair of legs, armpits, mustache, beard, eyebrows, or eyelashes. But lice that live on the scalp are not pubic lice. They are head lice.

Crabs are usually transmitted through sexual contact. The little creatures can move from the pubic hair of one person to that of another. In fact, people can even get the disease just by "fooling around" without having intercourse. Crabs can also be spread by sleeping in an infested bed, using infested towels, or wearing infested clothes. That is because they can live one to two days without a human host. But they *cannot* be caught from a toilet. They dry out and die there.

Once pubic lice are on a person's body, they survive by sucking blood from their host. It is not easy to see these tiny insects because their tan to grayish color makes them blend into their surroundings. But they often lay eggs called nits, which may be more noticeable. (They look like tiny white blobs.) People with crabs may have intense itching in the pubic area, especially at

The Life Cycle of Lice

Pubic lice go through three stages of life: nit, nymph, and adult.

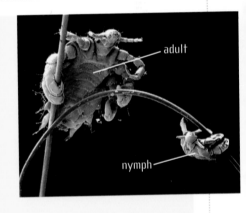

Nit: Nits are pubic lice eggs. They are white blobs, attached firmly to the hair.

Nymph: The nit hatches into a nymph. A nymph looks like an adult, only smaller. A nymph takes seven days to become an adult. Then it has to feed on blood.

Adult: The adult looks like a tiny crab. It has six legs, but the two front legs are very large and look like a crab's pincer claws. The adult is tan to gray.

night. The itching is caused by the crabs' bites, just as mosquito bites make people itch. Having crabs does not cause any serious health problems, but it makes living very uncomfortable. Roughly 3 million people in the United States suffer from crabs.[5]

Crabs are diagnosed by looking for nits, nymphs, or adult pubic lice. People may be able to see them using a strong magnifying glass. If they are not sure, they should see a doctor. A microscope may be needed to identify them properly.

Crabs can be treated successfully. Special shampoos for killing lice are available in drugstores. Medicated shampoos or lotions are also available by prescription from a doctor. Even after treatment, nits are often still attached to the hair. They can be removed by running a fine-tooth comb through the hair. The person should also change into clean clothes, and all bedding should be removed and washed after treatment.

9

Preventing STDs

JACKIE WAS RECENTLY DIAGNOSED with chlamydia. She had been with only two men in her life. She had dated one of them for three years until they broke up a few months earlier. The other was her new boyfriend. Jackie didn't know which one had infected her. She was really afraid to tell either of them. She even thought about not telling them. After all, she had heard that chlamydia doesn't cause any serious problems in men. Jackie didn't know what to do, so she called an STD hotline. The person on the phone told her that she should tell all of her partners that she had chlamydia and that they should get tested. Not telling them would allow the disease to spread to other people. This could be dangerous, especially since chlamydia can lead to PID in women. Jackie asked what PID was, and the woman explained that it can damage the reproductive organs. Now Jackie knew what she had to do. She had to tell her partners, both past and present.[1]

Many STDs do not have a cure. People who are infected with herpes or HIV, for example, are infected for life. As mentioned earlier, having an STD increases the risk of developing AIDS, the deadliest of the STDs. Therefore, prevention is the *best* way to fight STDs.

Who's At Risk?

Anyone can get STDs, but certain groups of people have a greater chance of getting an STD because of their risky behaviors. These behaviors include:

- Having many different sex partners
- Intravenous drug use (when needles are shared)
- Sexual activity without protection (condom or dental dam)
- History of STDs

STD Vaccines?

Wouldn't it be nice to have a vaccine to protect us against STDs, like we have for polio or tetanus? Unfortunately, there is no single shot that can protect people against all STDs. In fact, a vaccine is available for only one of the major STDs so far—hepatitis B. Researchers are working on a number of others, which may be ready for general use within the next few years.

At first the hepatitis B vaccine was used just for people at high risk, such as health care workers who might be exposed to the blood of infected patients, injection drug users, people with multiple sex partners, and sex partners of hepatitis B carriers. Then health experts recommended that all children receive the vaccine routinely. Some parents objected, asking why *babies* needed to be immunized against a sexually transmitted disease. The reason is that hepatitis B is not only an STD; it can also be transmitted by contact with blood or other body fluids. There have even been cases of young children in day care centers being infected when another child bit them. (The virus is present in a carrier's saliva.) If a large part of the population is protected, chances of infection are greatly reduced. If vaccination is widespread enough, we may even be able

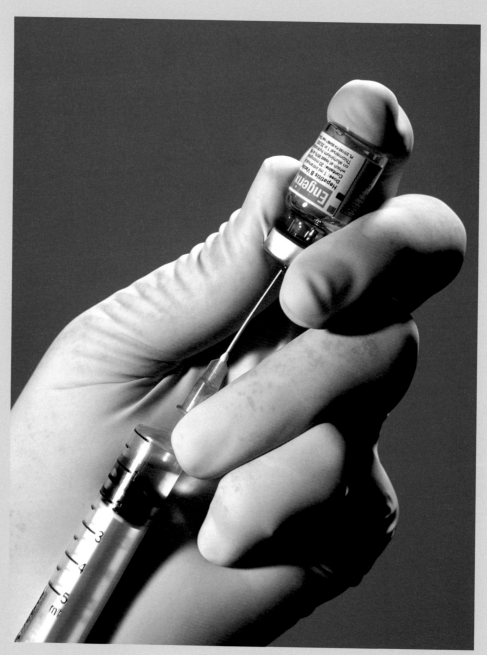

Hepatitis B vaccine.

to wipe out this disease completely. Now hepatitis B vaccination is one of the recommended immunizations for infants and young children. The vaccine is given in a series of three shots.

In 2004, wide-scale testing of Herpevac, a new vaccine against genital herpes, was begun at more than twenty medical facilities in the United States. More than 7,500 healthy female volunteers, ages eighteen to thirty, received the vaccine. Earlier tests had shown that Herpevac prevents infection in about 48 percent of uninfected women, but it prevents outbreaks in 74 percent of women already infected with herpes. Even with this limited success, health researchers calculate that widespread use of the vaccine could reduce the rate of herpes infection in both sexes by 40 percent in twenty-five years.

Some STD experts are skeptical about how widely such a vaccine would be accepted. Tamara Kreinin, president of the Sexuality Information and Education Council of the U.S., based in New York City, points out that high schools have begun offering hepatitis B vaccinations. However, she says, "the shame and stigma that surround herpes" could make a similar program for herpes less successful. "Girls lining up to get their

Two for One

The big recent success story on the STD front is a vaccine against human papillomavirus (HPV). It not only protects against this common STD, it is also the first successful vaccine to prevent cancer. The first version of the vaccine, announced in November 2002 by the drug company Merck, was found in clinical tests to be 100 percent effective against a strain of HPV that causes about half of all cervical cancers. Not one of the women who received the vaccine developed an HPV infection or any precancerous cells in the cervix. A newer vaccine, targeted against more strains of HPV, was expected to be on the market by 2006. This vaccine would provide protection not only against cervical cancer but also against genital warts in both men and women.[2]

shots could be fearful about being seen," she says. "Or they may never line up, mistakenly thinking, 'This disease is for [girls] who run around a lot—not for someone like me.'"[3]

Researchers are also working on an oral vaccine for chlamydia.

Several groups of AIDS researchers have been trying to develop vaccines against HIV. This has proven to be very difficult, mainly because the virus changes each time it reproduces. Tests of a number of vaccines are planned or already under way, but it will probably be many years before an AIDS vaccine is available.[4]

How Can We Protect Ourselves?

The only sure way to prevent STDs is abstinence. Abstinence means having no sex at all. Many young people today feel pressured to have sex. They have to deal not only with the pull of their own hormones, but also with the need to feel accepted and to please the one they love. People who think they are ready to have sex

The only sure way to prevent STDs is abstinence.

Abstinence means having no sex at all.

need to consider all the possible consequences. They may choose not to have sex. Or they may choose to use contraceptives, devices that can prevent pregnancy and some STDs as well.

A popular way to protect against STDs is using a condom. A condom is a thin, rubber covering that is

People who are dating should understand that abstinence is the only sure way to prevent STDs.

placed over an erect penis and collects the semen when a man ejaculates. Condoms are usually effective when used properly. They are not foolproof, however, because they can break. A spermicide can also be used with the condom for extra protection—spermicides kill some viruses and bacteria. Condoms do not protect against all STDs, however. For example, condoms do not prevent the spread of genital warts and crabs. Other kinds of contraceptives, such as birth-control pills, may prevent pregnancy but do *not* protect against diseases.

When properly used, condoms usually prevent STDs.

Even for those who are abstinent or who always use protection when having sex, it is important to see a doctor regularly. Women should see a gynecologist every year. Men should have annual physicals. For most STDs, early detection is important for treatment—and to prevent further spread of the disease.

When it comes to sex, what you don't know can hurt you. Sex is not all fun and games. It is a big responsibility, and one that can have unwanted consequences. Be smart about sex and know your sex partner. Remember that when you have sex with someone, you are having sex with every person he or she has ever had sex with.

Questions and Answers

I have just been diagnosed with syphilis. I thought people don't get that disease anymore. Is it still deadly like it was centuries ago? Syphilis can be very dangerous if it's not caught early. Fortunately, these days antibiotics can treat the disease successfully.

I've been with only one guy, but I just found out that I have an STD. Has my boyfriend been cheating on me? Not necessarily. Some STDs can hide out in the body for weeks, months, or even years until they produce symptoms. It is possible that your boyfriend was infected before you started dating him.

My boyfriend and I aren't having *real* sex, just oral sex. Do I have to worry about getting an STD? Yes. STDs can be spread by oral sex, as well as by sexual intercourse. You're still coming into contact with your partner's genitals and body fluids. If he is infected, he can pass it on to you.

My mom always told me never to sit on a public toilet seat. That's how diseases are spread. Can I get an STD that way? No. The germs that cause STDs cannot survive for long on a toilet seat. Pubic lice can live for an hour or two on towels, clothes, and bedding, but they cannot survive on toilet seats. They dry out and die.

When my mom found out that my boyfriend and I were "doing it," she took me to the doctor to get a prescription for the pill. Does that protect me from STDs? No. The pill just protects against unwanted pregnancy. It does not prevent STDs. Condoms provide protection against bacterial and viral STDs, but even condoms aren't perfect. And they don't provide any protection against genital warts or pubic lice.

My ex-boyfriend gave me herpes. They say "herpes is forever." Does that mean I can never have sex again, without putting my partner at risk? Can I ever get married and have children? People with herpes can live normal lives, as long as they are careful. There are medicines that can prevent outbreaks or make them less severe. Many people with herpes are living in long-term relationships without infecting their partners. A mother may transmit the infection to her unborn child during pregnancy, though.

I just had a blood test that came back positive for chlamydia. But I feel fine. How can I have a disease?

Many people with chlamydia do not have any symptoms. However, the germs can cause trouble later. In women, the disease can lead to pelvic inflammatory disease (PID), a condition that can damage the reproductive organs. If you have chlamydia, you need to get treatment.

STDs Timeline

1493 .... Syphilis first appears in Europe.

1530 .... Girolamo Fracastoro writes a poem about a shepherd named Syphilus; his name is borrowed for the disease.

*pherd once (dis.
ossest these Downs, an
Some destin'd Head t'attor.
On Syphilus the dreadful Lo
Through what adventures t
So lately did astonisht Eur
Through Asian coasts and
from what Seeds*

1540 .... Gonorrhea first appears in Europe.

1837 .... French STD specialist Philippe Ricord proves that gonorrhea and syphilis are actually two different diseases (contrary to popular belief at the time).

1905 .... German scientists Fritz Schaudinn and Erich Hoffman discover that syphilis is caused by the spirochete, *Treponema pallidum.*

1909 .... Paul Ehrlich and Sukehachiro Hata discover Salvarsan, the first effective treatment for syphilis.

1928 .... Alexander Fleming discovers the antibiotic penicillin, which will replace Salvarsan as the most effective treatment for syphilis.

1950s	Penicillin becomes widely available for STDs.
1981	The first AIDS cases are reported in the United States; vaccine against hepatitis B is approved by the FDA.
1982	The term *AIDS* is adopted for the new immune deficiency syndrome.
1985	The first antibody tests for AIDS are developed.
1987	AZT, the first effective drug against AIDS, is approved by the FDA.
1991	The CDC recommends that infants be vaccinated against hepatitis B.
1996	Three-drug treatment for AIDS is proposed by David Ho.
2002	Clinical tests of the first vaccine against human papillomavirus are successful.
2004	Widespread clinical testing of Herpevac begins.

For More Information

Organizations

American Liver Foundation
75 Maiden Lane, Suite 603
New York, NY 10038-4810
1-800-465-4837
<http://www.liverfoundation.org>

American Social Health Association (ASHA)
P.O. Box 13827
Research Triangle Park, NC 27713
1-919-361-8400
<http://www.ashastd.org>

Centers for Disease Control and Prevention
1600 Clifton Road, NE
Atlanta, GA 30333
1-404-639-3534
Toll free: 1-800-311-3435
<http://www.cdc.gov/>

National Institute of Allergy and Infectious Diseases
6610 Rockledge Drive, MSC 6612
Bethesda, MD 20892-6612
<http://www.niaid.nih.gov/publications/stds.htm>

Hotlines

Gay Men's Health Crisis (GMHC)
1-212-807-6655

National Herpes Hotline
1-919-361-8488

National HIV/AIDS Hotline
1-800-342-AIDS (1-800-342-2437)

National STD Hotline
1-800-227-8922

Chapter Notes

Chapter 1. What's Wrong With Sex?

1. Tamar Nordenberg, "Chlamydia's Quick Cure," *FDA Consumer*, July–August 1999, pp. 24–28.

2. CDC National Prevention Information Network, "STDs Today," May 25, 2004, <http://cdcnpin.org/ scripts/ std/std.asp> (November 2, 2004).

3. Nemours Foundation, "About Sexually Transmitted Diseases (STDs)," © 1995–2004, <http:// kidshealth.org/teen/sexual_health/stds/std.html> (November 2, 2004).

4. Health Square, "Sexually Transmitted Diseases (STDs)," ©2004, <http://www.healthsquare.com/ ftstd.htm> (November 2, 2004).

5. Nemours Foundation.

Chapter 2. Hijacking the Reproductive System

1. Ben Waggoner, "Antony van Leeuwenhoek," August 25, 1996, <http://www.ucmp.berkeley.edu/ history/leeuwenhoek.html> (November 2, 2004).

Chapter 3. Syphilis

1. Adapted from Shriya Dave, Deepthy V. Gopinath, and Devinder M. Thappa, "Nodular Secondary Syphilis," *Dermatology Online Journal*, vol. 9, no. 1, 2003, <http://dermatology.cdlib.org/91/case_reports/ syphilis/thappa.html> (November 2, 2004).

2. "United States STD Statistics," <http://www. avert.org/stdstatisticusa.htm> (September 2, 2004;

updated December 15, 2004), taken from CDC document, "Sexually Transmitted Disease Surveillance Report, 2003" (March 17, 2005).

3. "Prevalence and Incidence of Syphilis," June 18, 2003, <http://www.wrongdiagnosis.com/s/syphilis/prevalence.htm> (March 22, 2005).

4. "Facts on Syphilis," <http://www.cdc.gov/std/media/FactsSyph11-28-01.htm> (November 28, 2001; modified August 4, 2004), CDC media release (March 17, 2005).

Chapter 4. Gonorrhea

1. John Sedgwick, "Beware of STDs," *Self*, July 1995, pp. 99–102, 139.

2. CDC: National Center for HIV, STD, and TB Prevention, "Gonorrhea Fact Sheet," August 4, 2004, <http://www.cdc.gov/std/Gonorrhea/STDFact-gonorrhea.htm> (November 2, 2004).

3. Nevada State Health Division, "Gonorrhea: Gonococcal Infection (clap, drip)," February 21, 2001 <http://health2k.state.nv.us/disease/diseases/gonorrhea.htm> (July 12, 2005).

4. National Institute of Allergy and Infectious Diseases, "Gonorrhea, NIAID Fact Sheet," October 2004, <http://www.niaid.nih.gov/factsheets/stdgon.htm> (November 2, 2004).

Chapter 5. Chlamydia

1. Adapted from "Spouse's Fidelity Uninvolved in Latent Chlamydia," *Newark Star Ledger*, September 19, 1990, p. 49.

2. National Institute of Allergy and Infectious Diseases, "Chlamydia Fact Sheet," July 2004, <http://www.niaid.nih.gov/factsheets/stdclam.htm> (November 2, 2004).

3. The Cleveland Clinic, "Chlamydia," October 2003, <http://my.webmd.com/content/article/46/2953_512.htm> (September 30, 2004).

4. Centers for Disease Control and Prevention, "Chlamydia Fact Sheet," <http://www.cdc.gov/std/Chlamydia/STDFact-Chlamydia.htm> (May 2004; updated February 25, 2005).

Chapter 6. Herpes

1. Adapted from Linda Bren, "Genital Herpes: A Hidden Epidemic," *FDA Consumer*, March–April 2002, p. 10.

2. Ibid., pp. 10–16.

3. Ibid., p. 10.

4. National Institute of Allergy and Infectious Diseases, *Genital Herpes Fact Sheet*, September 2003, <http://www.niaid.nih.gov/factsheets/stdherp.htm> (October 28, 2004).

5. Bren, p. 13.

Chapter 7. HIV and AIDS

1. Planned Parenthood Federation of America, Inc., "It Can't Happen to Me! Famous Last Words #1," ©1998–2004, <http://www.plannedparenthood.org/sti/itcant_page2.html> (November 3, 2004).

2. National Institute of Allergy and Infectious Diseases, "HIV/AIDS Statistics," July 2004, <http://www.niaid.nih.gov/factsheets/aidsstat.htm> (November 18, 2004).

3. Donald G. McNeil, Jr., "On Stages and Screens, AIDS Educators Reach South Africa's Youths," Health Systems Trust, from a *New York Times* article, February 3, 2002, Section 1, page 6, <http://new.hst.org.za/news/index.php/ 20020212/> (March 19, 2005).

4. Will Weissert, "Drugs Given Away by AIDS Patients in U.S. Prolong Lives Worldwide," June 12, 2004, <http://www.aegis.org/news/ap/2004/ AP040628.html> (November 18, 2004).

Chapter 8. Other STDs

1. Lauren Picker, "Prevent Sexually Transmitted Diseases," *American Health*, October 1995, pp. 62–66.

2. National Institute of Allergy and Infectious Diseases, "Human Papillomavirus and Genital Warts Fact Sheet," July 2004, <http://www.niaid.nih.gov/fact-sheets/stdhpv.htm> (November 18, 2004).

3. Lisa Marr, M.D., *Sexually Transmitted Diseases: A Physician Tells You What You Need to Know*, Baltimore, MD: The Johns Hopkins University Press, 1998, p. 183.

4. Centers for Disease Control and Prevention, "STD Facts—Trichomoniasis," August 4, 2004, <http://www.cdc.gov/std/Trichomonas/STDFact-Trichomoniasis.htm> (November 18, 2004).

5. American Social Health Association, "Facts & Answers about STDs: Crabs," ©2001, <http://www.ashastd.org/stdfaqs/crabs.html> (September 14, 2004).

Chapter 9. Preventing STDs

1. Adapted from Sherry Amatenstein, "Dating Doyenne: How Do I Tell Him That I Have an STD?" October 6, 2000; rev. February 21, 2002, <http://www.ivillage.com/relationships/experts/dating/qas/0,,182410_98391,00.html?arrivalSA=1&cobrandRef=0&arrival_freqCap=2> (November 18, 2004).

2. Kerry Capell and Amy Barrett, "A Vaccine Every Woman Should Take," *Business Week*, November 29, 2004, p. 54.

3. Molly M. Ginty, "Herpes Vaccine Might Protect Female Teens," *Women's eNews*, November 16, 2004, Run Date March 7, 2004, <http://www.womensenews.org/article.cfm/dyn/aid/1741/context/archive> (November 26, 2004).

4. Emilio A. Emini and Wayne C. Koff, "Developing an AIDS Vaccine: Need, Uncertainty, Hope," *Science*, June 25, 2004, pp. 1913–1914.

Glossary

abstinence—Not having sex at all.

antibodies—Proteins that are produced to attach specifically to surface chemicals on an invading virus.

antigen—A chemical that stimulates antibody production.

antiviral drugs—Medicine that kills certain viruses.

carrier—A person who is infected by a disease germ but does not have any symptoms; the person can spread the disease to other people.

cervix—The entrance to the uterus.

chancre (*pronounced* SHANG-ker)—A sore produced by syphilis.

chlamydia—The most common STD; caused by the bacterium *Chlamydia trachomatis*.

condom—A thin rubber covering placed over the penis during sexual intercourse to prevent pregnancy and the spread of disease.

contraceptive—A device or drug used to prevent pregnancy or the spread of diseases.

discharge—Liquid that flows from a body opening, such as the penis or vagina.

disseminated gonorrhea—Gonorrhea that has spread to other parts of the body, affecting those other body parts.

drug resistance—Ability of a disease germ to survive and multiply in the presence of a drug that would ordinarily kill or disable it.

ectopic pregnancy—A pregnancy in which the fertilized egg develops outside the womb, such as in a fallopian tube. The fetus cannot survive, and even the mother's life is in danger when this happens.

ejaculation—Passage of semen out of the body through the penis.

epidemic—An infectious disease that spreads to many people.

erection—Enlargement and stiffening of the penis.

fallopian tube—One of a pair of tubes that grow out from the "horns" of the uterus, with open ends near the ovaries.

fertilization—The joining of an egg and a sperm that produces an offspring.

genes—Chemical units that determine hereditary traits passed on from one generation to the next.

genital—Pertaining to one of the sex organs (male or female; also called genital organs or reproductive organs).

genital herpes—An STD caused by a virus that produces sores and blisters on the sex organs; outbreaks tend to recur.

genital warts—An STD caused by the human

papillomavirus (HPV) that produces cauliflower-like growths in the genital area.

gonorrhea—A common STD nicknamed "the clap"; caused by the bacterium *Neisseria gonorrhoeae*.

helper T cells—White blood cells that help other cells of the immune system to make antibodies.

hepatitis B—An STD caused by a virus that attacks the liver; it can be spread through contact with blood as well as sexually.

heterosexual—A person who is attracted to persons of the opposite sex.

homosexual—A person who is attracted to persons of the same sex.

host—A living plant or animal that provides food and shelter for another creature.

human immunodeficiency virus (HIV)—The virus that attacks the immune system and eventually leads to AIDS.

human papillomavirus (HPV)—A virus that causes warts.

immune system—The body's disease-fighting system, which includes the white blood cells, interferon, and many other chemicals.

infertility—The inability to have children.

inflammation—Swelling, pain, heat, and redness in the tissues around a site of infection.

Kaposi's sarcoma—A skin cancer that produces purplish spots.

menstrual cycle—The female reproductive process, including ripening and releasing of an egg, thickening of the lining of the uterus, and a flow of blood due to breakdown of the uterine lining if the egg has not been fertilized. The complete process is repeated about once a month.

menstruation—The flow of blood that occurs in an adult female about once a month, when the lining of the uterus breaks down after an egg has passed out of the body without being fertilized.

microorganisms—Any organisms that cannot be seen by the naked eye.

monogamous—Having only one sex partner at a time.

nits—Eggs laid by lice, usually glued to hair.

opportunistic infections—Illnesses caused by viruses or bacteria that live in the body but do not normally make people sick.

ovary (*plural* **ovaries**)—One of a pair of female sex organs, in which eggs are produced and stored and hormones are secreted.

ovulation—The release of a ripe egg from an ovary.

pelvic inflammatory disease (PID)—A complication resulting usually from gonorrhea or chlamydia that damages a woman's fallopian tubes or uterus.

penis—The male sex organ used to transfer sperm to the female during sexual intercourse. It is also used for urination.

prodrome—A tingling or itching feeling in the genital area, or pain in the buttocks, down the legs, or in the lower back, that occurs before other disease symptoms appear.

pubic lice—An STD commonly called "crabs"; caused by tiny insects that infest the hair in the genital areas; can be transmitted through contact sexually or through infected clothing or bedding.

recurrence—The return of symptoms that had gone into hiding.

scrotum—The loose bag of skin containing the testes.

semen—The fluid containing sperm.

septic arthritis—An infection of the joints by gonorrhea bacteria, resulting in pain and stiffness.

sex organ—A body part used for reproduction; also called genital organs or genitals.

sexual intercourse—Sexual activity involving contact of the genitals.

sexually transmitted disease (STD)—Any disease that can be transferred from one partner to another usually as a result of vaginal, oral, or anal sex.

sperm—A male sex cell.

syphilis—An STD caused by the spirochete *Treponema pallidum*; progresses through three or four stages.

testicle (*plural* **testicles** *or* **testes**)—One of a pair of male sex organs in which sperm are produced.

trichomoniasis—An STD caused by a protozoa.

urethra—A passage that carries urine from the bladder to the outside of the body; in males, it also carries semen.

uterus—The organ in which a fertilized egg grows into a baby; the womb.

vagina—A passage leading from the uterus to the outside of the body.

vesicles—Fluid-filled blisters.

vulva—The external parts of the female sex organs.

Further Reading

Hunter, Miranda and William. *Staying Safe: A Teen's Guide to Sexually Transmitted Diseases*. Philadelphia: Mason Crest Publishers, 2005.

Tocci, Salvatore. *Sexually Transmitted Diseases*. New York: Franklin Watts, 2001.

Woods, Samuel G. *Everything You Need to Know About: STDs (Sexually Transmitted Diseases)*. New York: The Rosen Publishing Group, Inc., 2003.

Yancy, Diane. *STDs: What You Don't Know Can Hurt You*. Brookfield, Conn.: Twenty-First Century Books, 2002.

Internet Addresses

(See also **For More Information**, p. 110.)

American Social Health Association. "Answers to Your Questions About Teen Sexual Health and Sexually Transmitted Diseases." © 2005. <http://www.iwannaknow.org>

Nemours Foundation. *Teens Health*. "Sexually Transmitted Diseases (STDs)." <http://www.kidshealth.org/teen/sexual_health/stds/std.html>

Planned Parenthood. *Teenwire.com*. © 1999–2005. <http://www.teenwire.com>

Index

A

abstinence, 101
Aid to AIDS program, 78, 79
AIDS, 12, 13, 22, 68–81
    attitudes toward, 80–81
    diagnosis, 76–78
    education, 74
    statistics, 72
    symptoms, 75–76
    transmission, 73, 75
    treatment, 78–81
anal sex, 22
animalcules, 16
antibiotics, 47, 54
antibodies, 77, 87
antiviral drugs, 67, 80
anus, 22, 84

B

bacteria, 16, 18, 35, 40, 50
birth-control pills, 103
blindness, 34
blood, 73
blood transfusions, 73, 75
body fluids, 73
Borrelia burgdorferi, 32
breastfeeding, 73

C

cancer of the cervix, 84
carrier, 11, 87
cervix, 20, **21**, 42, 62, 84
chancre, 33
chlamydia, 9, **10**, 12, **16**, 22, 26,
    47, **48**, 49–56, 72, 95
    diagnosis, 53–54, 56

    statistics, **25**, 50–51, **52**
    symptoms, 51–53
    transmission, 51
    treatment, 51, 54
Chlamydia trachomatis, 50
clap. *See* gonorrhea.
Clemente, José, 78–79
cold sores, 61
condoms, 101, **103**
contraceptives, 101, 103
crabs. *See* pubic lice.

D

discharge, 44, 91
disseminated gonorrhea, 41–42
DNA, 46
drug resistance, 36, 47
drug users, **69**, 75

E

ectopic pregnancy, 43
ejaculation, 20
eye infection, 41, 51

F

fallopian tubes, 20, **21**, 42
female sex organs, 20, **21**
fertilization, 21
fever, 34, 42
Firstburst (test for chlamydia),
    54, **55**
Fracastoro, Girolamo, 30

G

genes, 77
genitals, 18, 41, 73

genital herpes, 60, 72
genital warts, 12, 24, 82, 84–85, 103
 treatment, 85
gonorrhea, 12, 22, 26, 38–47, 72
 diagnosis, 44–47
 statistics, 40, 41
 symptoms, 41–44
 transmission, 40
 treatment, 47
gonorrhea culture, 45, **46**
Gram's stain, 45
"great pox," 30
gynecologist, 104

H
helper T cells, 76–77
hepatitis B, 12, 85–88
 chronic, 87
 statistics, 86, 87
 symptoms, 88
 transmission, 86
 treatment, 88
hepatitis B vaccine, 97, **98**, 99
herpes, 12, 22, 24, 57–67
 diagnosis, 66
 recurrence, 64–65
 statistics, 59–61
 symptoms, 57, 62–63, 65
 transmission, 60–61
 treatment, 67
herpes simplex virus (HSV), 59, **62**, 66
Herpevac, 99–100
heterosexuals, 24
HIV, 68–81
 diagnosis, 76–78

statistics, 72
symptoms, 75–76
transmission, 72–73, 75
treatment, 78–81
HIV vaccine, 100–101
homosexuals, 24
host, 16, 18, 63, 75, 93
HSV-1, 59–61
HSV-2, 60, 61
human immunodeficiency virus. *See* HIV.
human papillomavirus (HPV), 83–84
 transmission, 83
 vaccine, 100

I
immune system, 71
infertility, 13, 43, 52
inflammation, 34

K
Kaposi's sarcoma, 76

L
Leeuwenhoek, Anton van, 15–16, **17**
liver, **85**, 89
Lyme disease, 32
lymph nodes, 34, 75, 76

M
male sex organs, **19**, 20
menstrual cycle, 21
menstruation, 21, 22
microorganisms, 17
microscope, 15–16, 35
monogamous relationship, 24